# FREE GOODIES

Dear Fantastic Parents,

Thank you for allowing your child to join me on this creative journey.

I wanted to share a tiny secret with you as a special surprise. You can access a treasure trove of practice pages for your child to explore, enjoy, and improve their lettering skills. And here's the best part: you can download and print these practice pages as much as you like, allowing your little one to practice to their heart's content!

Scan the QR code below to access these extra resources or go to our website at https://www.riccagarden.com/lettering-freebies-for-kids/.

Thank you for being such wonderful parents and encouraging your kid's imagination. Let's make this journey one to remember, full of lovely letters, creative designs, and never-ending inspiration!

With wagging tails and boundless creativity,

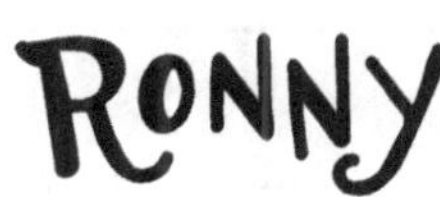


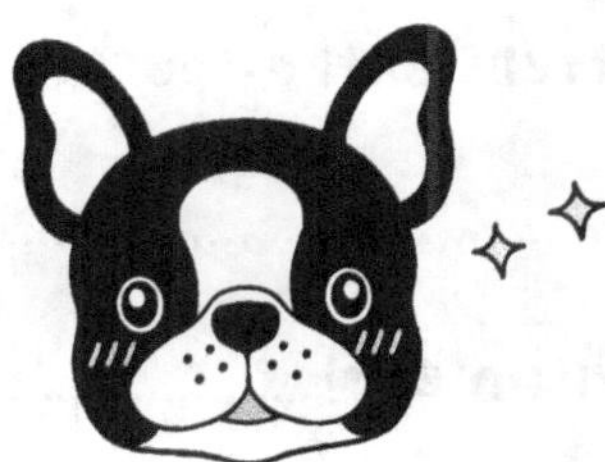

(Note: You must be 16 years or older, so grab your parents' help if you need.)

# TABLE OF CONTENTS

# THE Lettering Workbook for KIDS

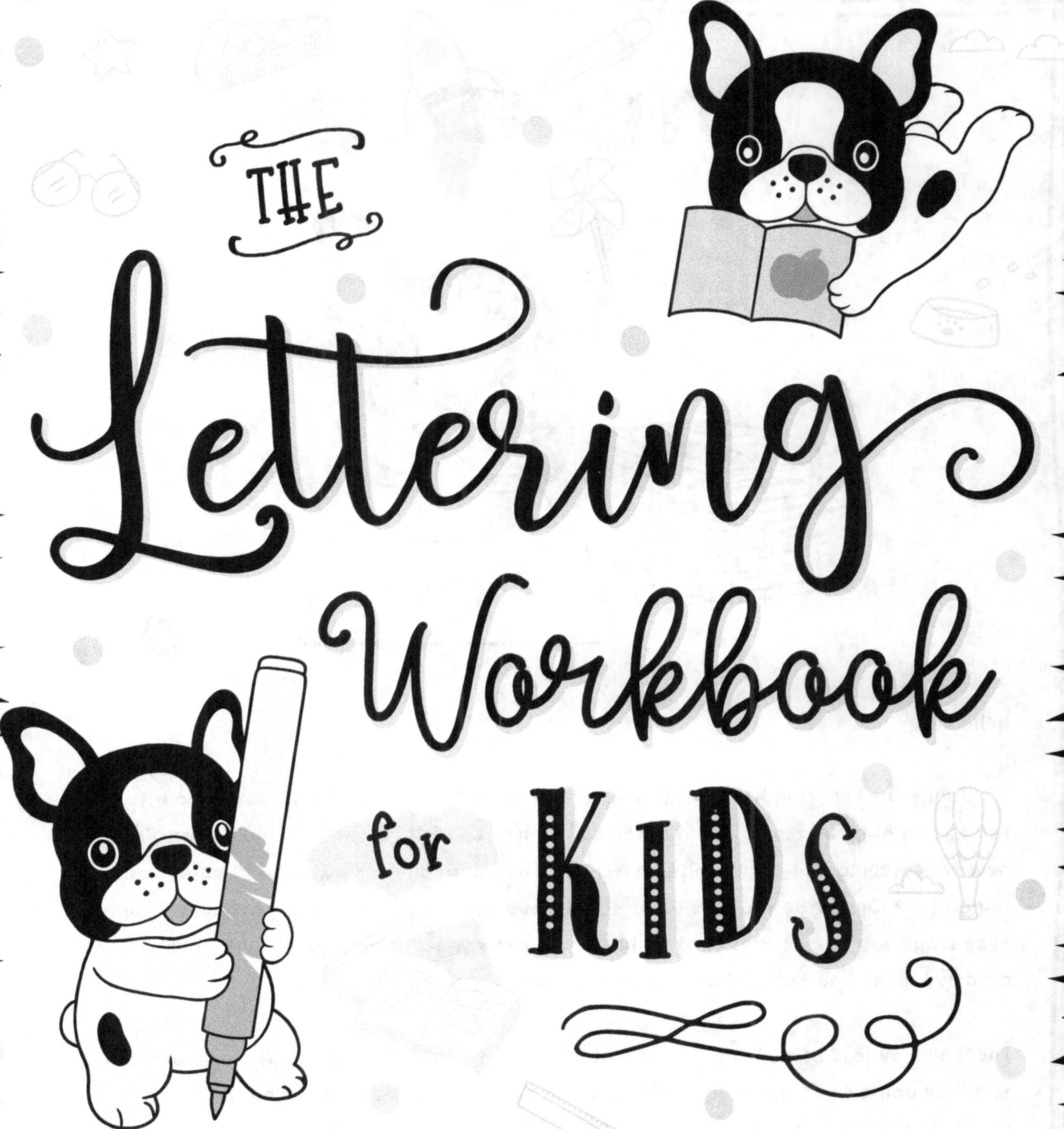

EXPLORE HAND LETTERING & MODERN CALLIGRAPHY

with

RONNY the FRENCHIE

# INTRODUCTION

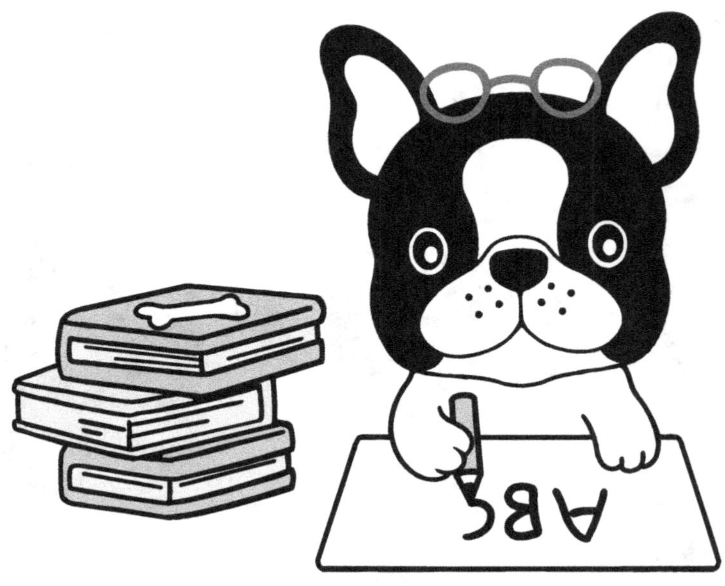


Hello kids!

It's Ronny the Frenchie here, your favorite bulldog. I can't wait to show you how fun and rewarding hand lettering and modern calligraphy can be! I wonder if you're completely new to lettering and calligraphy, or if you've had a go already but couldn't quite get the hang of it? Or maybe you just want to improve your handwriting in general. Well, whatever stage you are at, this book will help you get the techniques just right, give you cool creative ideas, and totally level up your writing style!

There will be lots of tips and fun activities to try too and, by the end of this workbook, you'll be doing some amazing stuff! Your new skills will come in super handy for making cards, journaling, writing old-school letters, school projects, and more.

But first, let me share with you a bit about how calligraphy evolved. I've had my nose to the ground, digging around on the subject, and it's just so interesting!

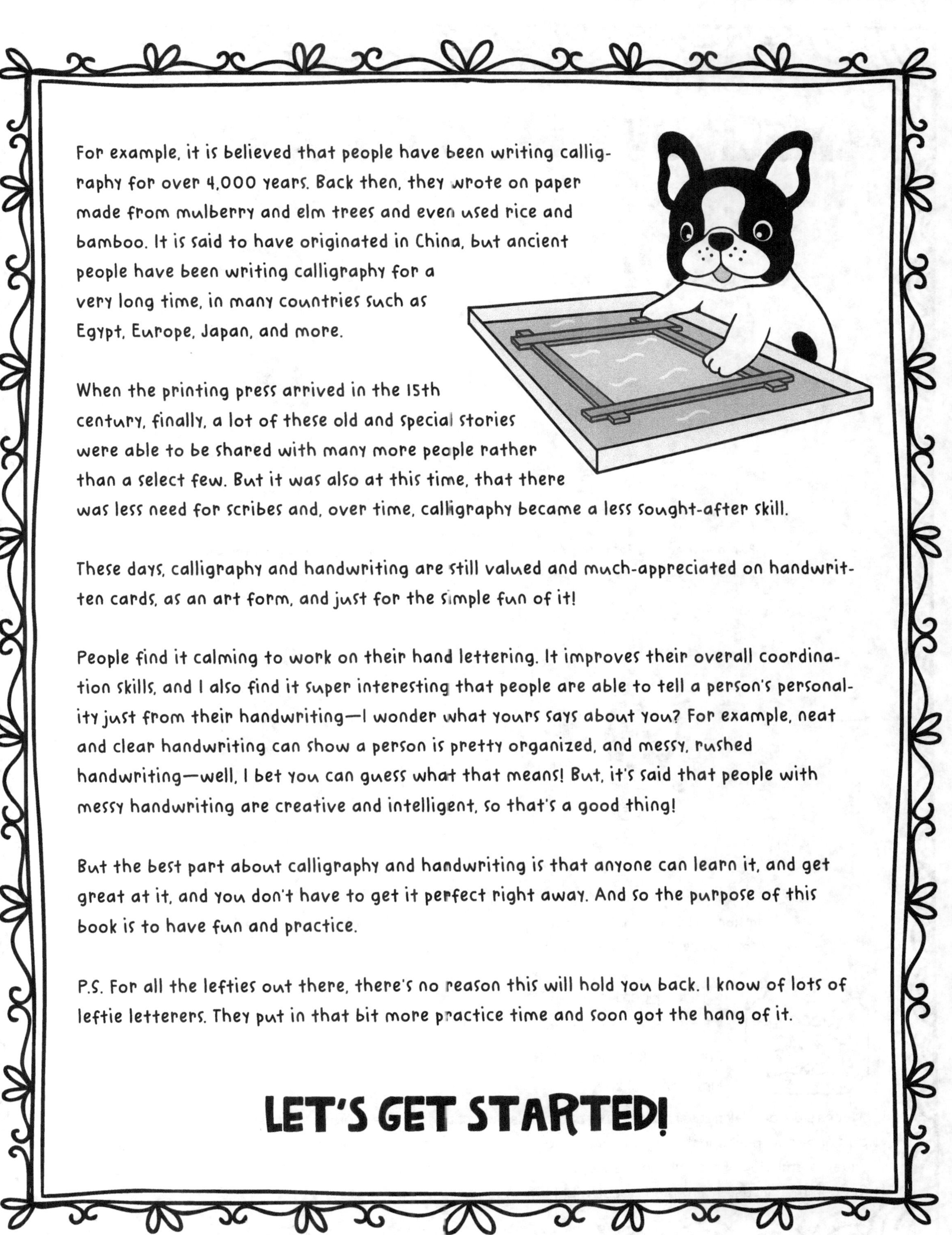

For example, it is believed that people have been writing calligraphy for over 4,000 years. Back then, they wrote on paper made from mulberry and elm trees and even used rice and bamboo. It is said to have originated in China, but ancient people have been writing calligraphy for a very long time, in many countries such as Egypt, Europe, Japan, and more.

When the printing press arrived in the 15th century, finally, a lot of these old and special stories were able to be shared with many more people rather than a select few. But it was also at this time, that there was less need for scribes and, over time, calligraphy became a less sought-after skill.

These days, calligraphy and handwriting are still valued and much-appreciated on handwritten cards, as an art form, and just for the simple fun of it!

People find it calming to work on their hand lettering. It improves their overall coordination skills, and I also find it super interesting that people are able to tell a person's personality just from their handwriting—I wonder what yours says about you? For example, neat and clear handwriting can show a person is pretty organized, and messy, rushed handwriting—well, I bet you can guess what that means! But, it's said that people with messy handwriting are creative and intelligent, so that's a good thing!

But the best part about calligraphy and handwriting is that anyone can learn it, and get great at it, and you don't have to get it perfect right away. And so the purpose of this book is to have fun and practice.

P.S. For all the lefties out there, there's no reason this will hold you back. I know of lots of leftie letterers. They put in that bit more practice time and soon got the hang of it.

# LET'S GET STARTED!

# CHECK OUT MY OTHER BOOKS!

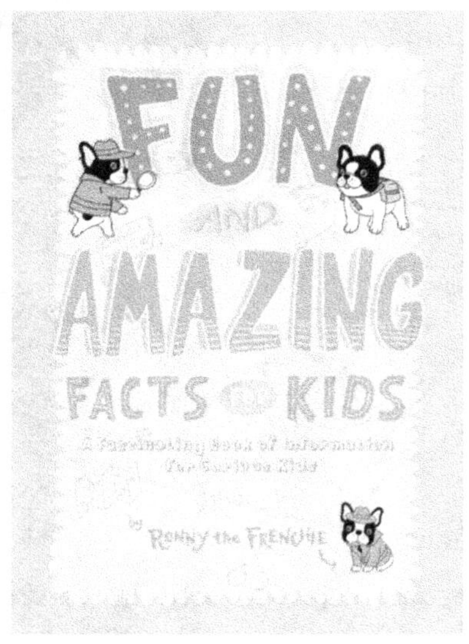


Fun and Amazing Facts for Kids

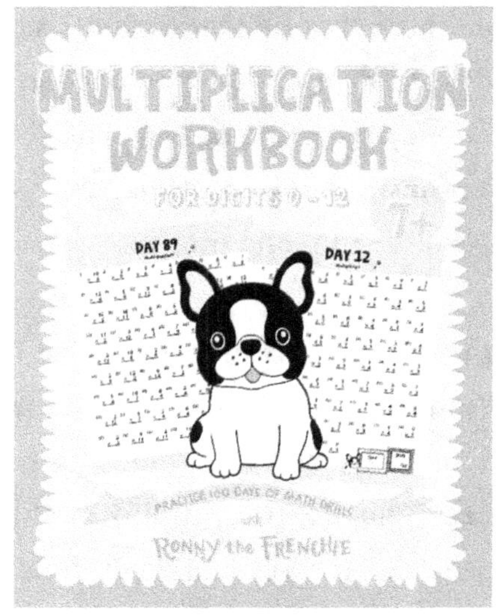


Multiplication Workbook for Digits 0 - 12

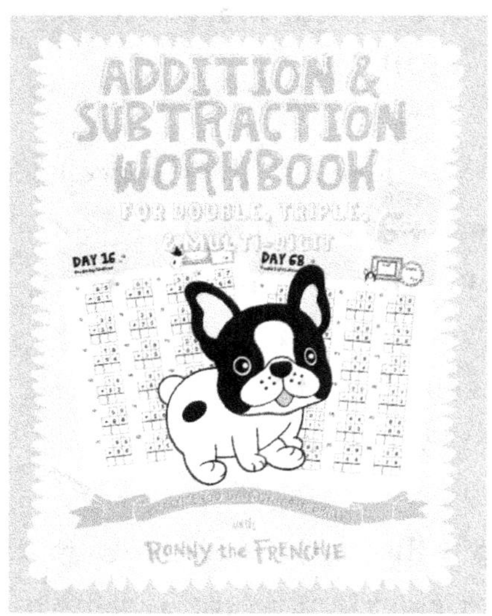


Addition and Subtraction Workbook
for Double, Triple, & Multi-Digit

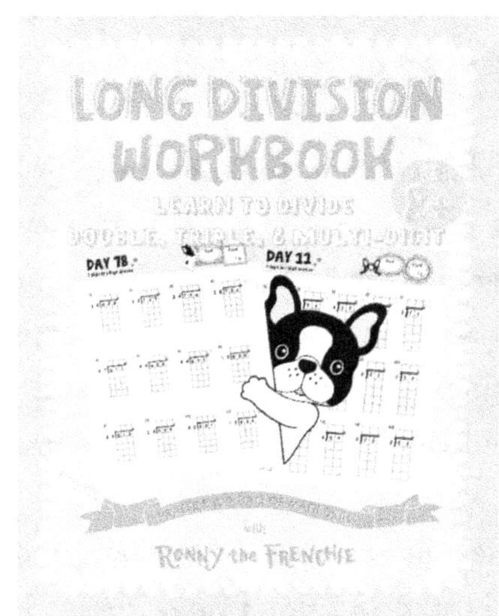


Long Division Workbook
Learn to Divide Double, Triple, & Multi-Digit

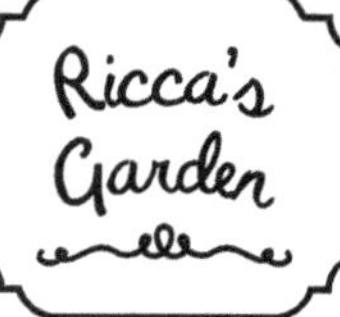


ricca_garden

info@riccagarden.com

Published & Designed in Brisbane, Australia

First Print: Jul 2023

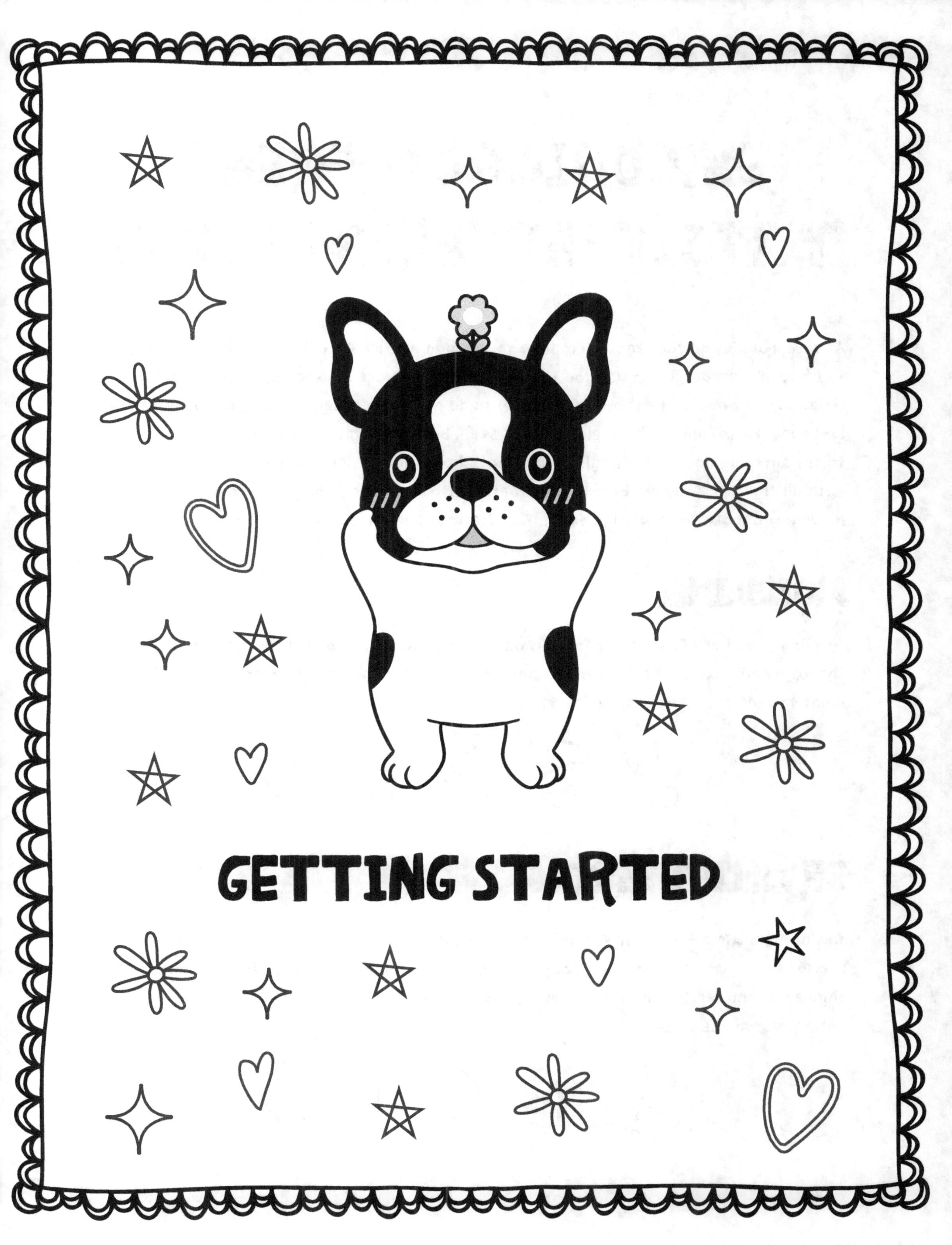
GETTING STARTED

# EXPLORING DIFFERENT TYPES OF LETTERING STYLES

As you probably already know, (I'm sure you've had a quick flick through the book! And if you haven't already, what are you waiting for?), there are a bunch of different lettering styles. In this book, I'll be showing you how to do many fun styles, such as: Monoline, Brush Lettering, Faux Calligraphy, Serif, and Sans Serif, but really anything goes, so don't be afraid to try anything and everything! I mean, that's how these styles started in the first place. As with all things, it's always best to get started with the basics and get them down pat, then move on to make your writing fancy, fun, special, or add your own style to it.

## MONOLINE

You don't need any fancy tools for this one. It's the same style and thickness all the way through and is used when you might have other interesting things going on around it and want to keep the writing style pretty basic.

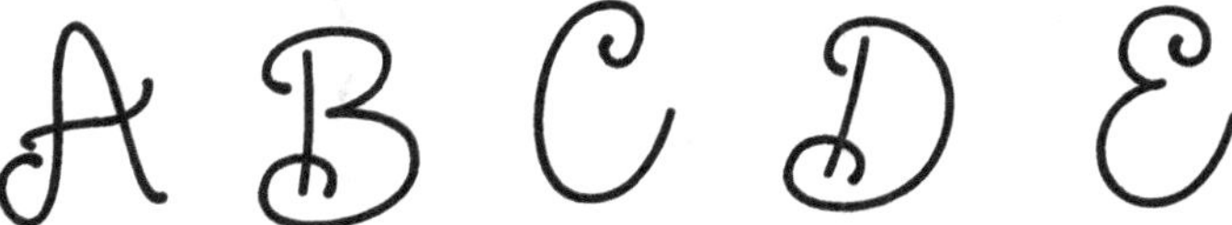


## BRUSH LETTERING

You need to use a brush pen for this one, which is so fun because the different levels of pressure you put on it (pressing down on the page) will give different results making it thinner or thicker. It can be a bit tricky, and you'll have to keep at it by practicing, but it's totally worth the effort!

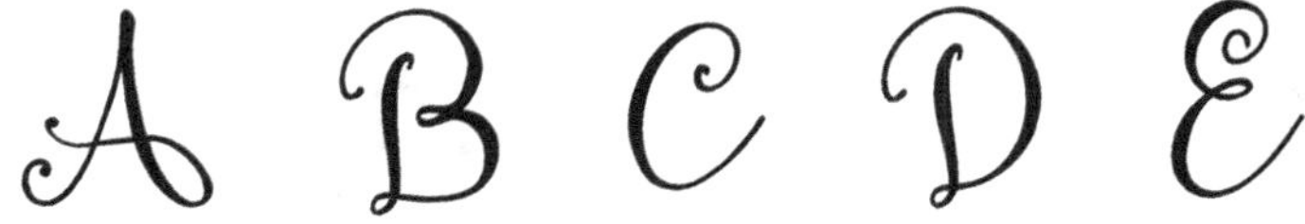

## FAUX CALLIGRAPHY

Faux Calligraphy is easier. It builds on what you've learned from the Monoline and Brush Lettering. Basically, you write in the Monoline style, but go back over it adding down-strokes to certain letters to give it that brush look without having to get the pressure just right.

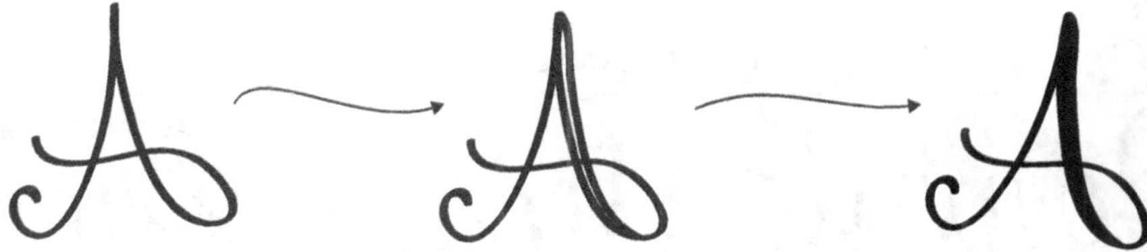


## SERIF

You can start getting a bit creative with this one by adding little bits to the ends of the letters, extending them, and adding some personality.

A B C D E

## SANS SERIF

Did you know that 'sans' means 'without' in French? Well, I do because I'm a Frenchie! So you can probably work out that this means not adding little bits to the end of the letters, giving the writing a fresh, simple, and modern look.

A B C D E

# TERMINOLOGY

There are a few basic words to learn that will come up from time to time. These words will help you to keep your writing the same throughout and to write better overall.

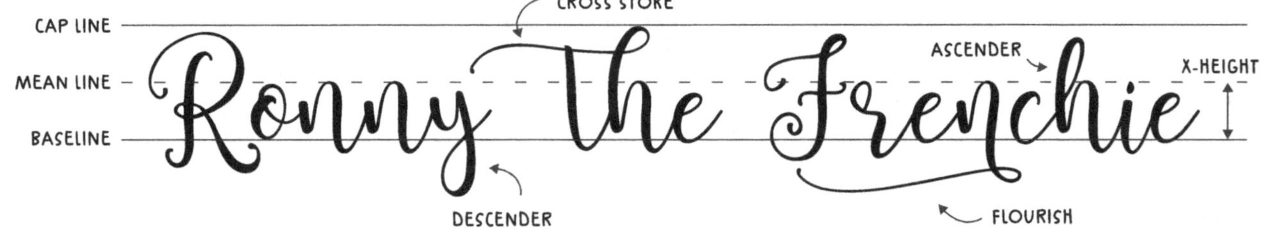


## BASELINE

It keeps you in line! I'm sure you've written something at some point and realized you've been leaning in one direction or it's all over the place. The baseline is where the letters stay and helps to keep them all in one spot so you don't get off track.

## MEAN LINE

Think 'M' for middle—this is your middle line, the imaginary spot where the tips of most of your lowercase letters will be. Keep in mind there are also letters like l, k, b, and d that do reach the cap line.

## X-HEIGHT

This is the distance between the baseline and the mean line (the height of the lowercase x).

## CAP LINE

'Cap' for capital letter—this line marks the top of the capital letter. I wonder why the lowercase one (above), is not called Low Line?!

## ASCENDER

Any part of the letter that is above the mean line is called an ascender.

## DESCENDER

I'm sure you can guess this one! Any part of the letter that is below the mean line is called a descender.

## DOWNSTROKE

The downstroke is the action of the pen going down, (obviously!) The downstroke is almost always thick (not as obvious!)

## UPSTROKE

You know this. The upstroke is the action of the pen going up, and is always thin.

## CROSS STROKE

This is a horizontal (straight-across) line that connects letters. For example, the cross on a 't'.

## FLOURISH

Flourishes are fun and where you decorate the letter, such as where you make the tail on a 'y' curly or long.

## LETTERFORM

This means the basic shape of the letter.

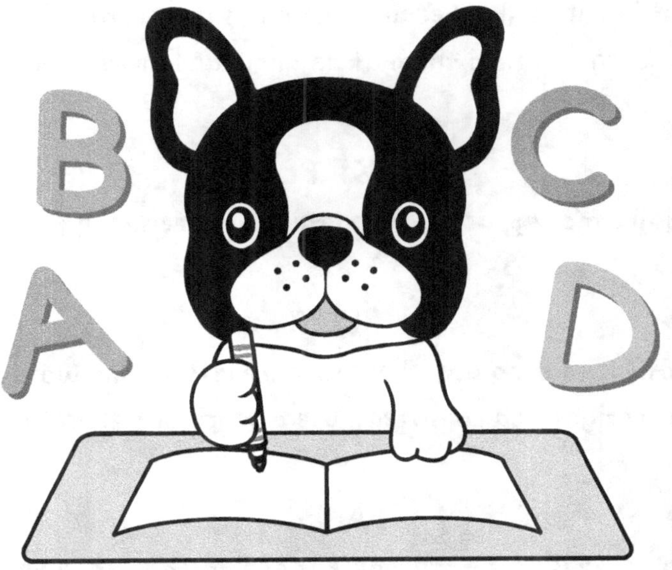

# TOOLS

Yay for all the fun tools!

Most of these tools you will already have but, I know, you may want to add a few more special bits and pieces as you go along and you may just want to check out that art shop, right?

## PENCILS

Handy for making lines to trace over and for sketching and practicing.

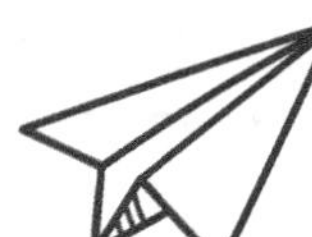

## COLORED PENCILS

Coloring details/shading.

## ERASER

Your BFF when practicing.

## PENS

Really fun for starting out and for the many different types you can get: from gel pens to thick and thin pens.

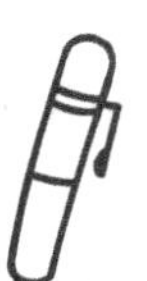

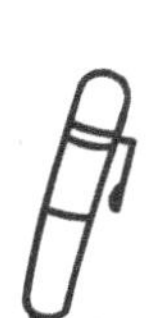

## MARKERS

There are so many types you can try out! And colored markers will make your letters stand out. Crayola broad line markers are great in particular because their tips can create thick and thin strokes when you hold them at an angle and apply different pressures.

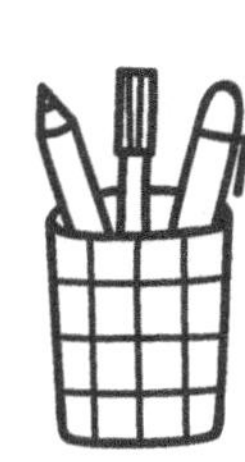

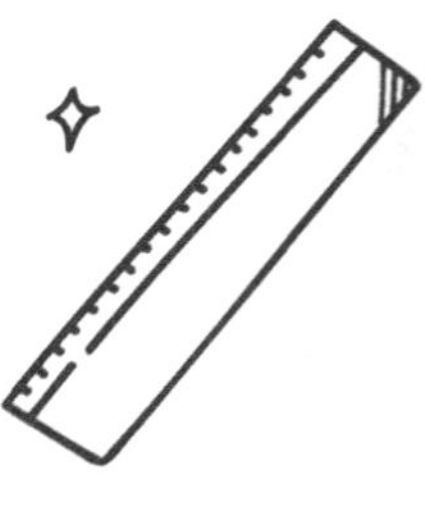

## BRUSH PENS

Require more practice to control but are super fun too!

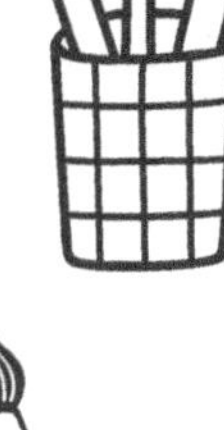

## RULER

Handy for making guidelines so your letters and words are nice and straight and consistent. Use a pencil and erase them later.

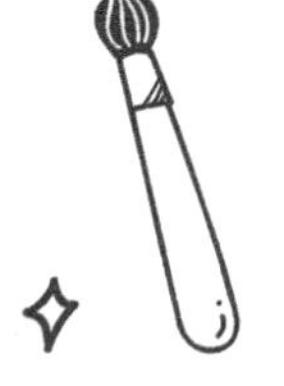

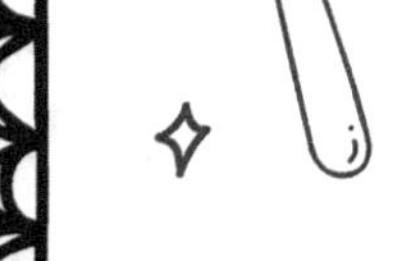

## PAPER

Smooth paper is best—otherwise it can damage your brush pens.

# POSITION AND POSTURE

So just like we don't want you slouched over your computer because it can cause neck or back problems, you must sit properly to write well and look after your body.

The ideal writing position and posture include sitting upright on a firm chair (not curled up on the couch), where your arm is, and how you hold the pen.

Tips:

- Sit at a desk—easy!
- I do want you sitting with your feet on the floor and not slouching, but not super-stiff either, because I want you to relax into the writing, have fun, and let your creativity flow out of your mind, down your arm, and flick across the page!

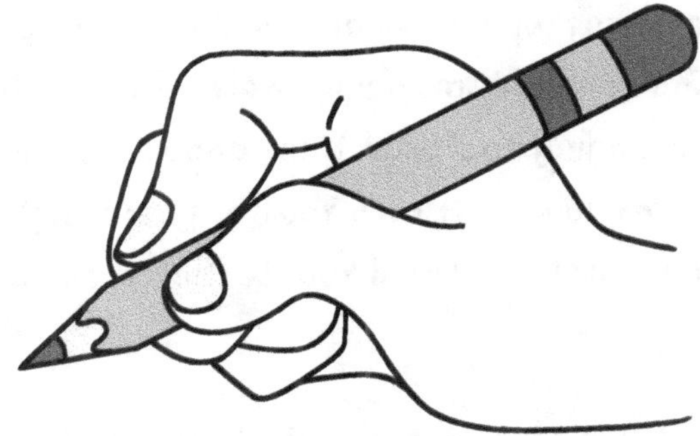

- Hold your pen (or whatever tool you're using) between your thumb and index finger, laying the pen on your middle finger, and leaning on a slanted angle (45 degrees to be exact! Yes, I told you I've been noseying around!)
- Don't grip it for dear life! It's not going anywhere, so hold it loosely because, again, I want you to be able to let it all flow, and have fun with it. You're not in school now. (Yay again!)
- It's handy to remember it's actually your arm that's doing most of the work, not your hand or fingers—they are just holding the pen in place.
- It's okay to experiment with your grip till you feel comfortable.

- Don't rush! You're not doing a test, so there's no need to hurry. Take all the time in the world. The whole point is to relax and have fun.
- The pen needs to be put down and picked up again, while you take your time with each letter and do one letter at a time.
- Keep your spacing in mind—the space between each letter needs to be the same. Otherwise, some words will look bunched up and your writing might look a little messy.

# MY TOP TIPS!

## 1. LOVELY LEFTIES, THIS IS FOR YOU!

Take some extra time to experiment with your grip, and a really cool tip is to put some tracing paper under your hand to avoid smudging. Wait a little in between letters for them to dry (helps minimize smudging too), and think about moving your page around-there are no rules at all that say you must keep your paper straight. Turn it this way or that or all around—whatever works. See I told you, Lefties, that I'd have you covered!

## 2. THE BEST ARTISTS GET THAT WAY BY PLAYING AROUND AND HAVING FUN.

So make sure you let yourself go, and anything goes! Does that rhyme? This Frenchie is multi-talented!

## 3. BE KIND—TO YOURSELF!

No one nails this first try! Have patience with yourself as you practice and experiment. Even when you feel it's not working, every bit of practice adds up and at some point it will all come together. It can help to think about how you would treat someone who is younger than you and learning. You'd be patient and encouraging, right? So treat yourself the same way.

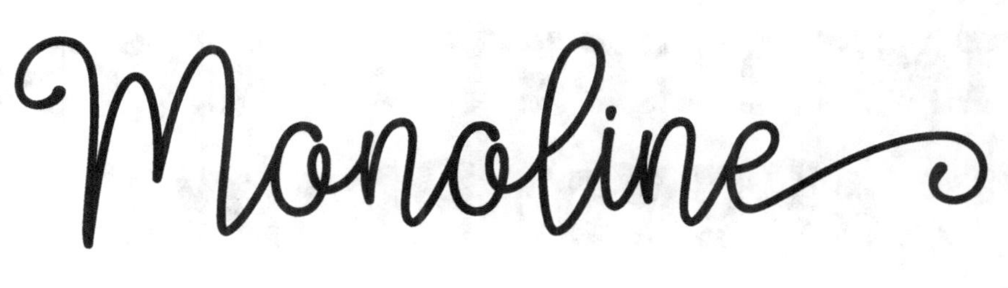


Let's learn the Monoline alphabet, which is simple and the thickness of the line stays the same all the way through—easy! It's handy and sometimes really important to have a more simple style so you can add whatever you like around it without it looking too fussy or messy.

Aa Bb Cc Dd Ee Ff Gg

Hh Ii Jj Kk Ll Mm Nn

Oo Pp Qq Rr Ss Tt Uu

Vv Ww Xx Yy Zz

You'll be able to spot Monoline on signs, advertising, or on your favorite logos. Once you get this one right, you're good to go. Play around a bit more with other styles, add your own signature flourish, mix up the slant angles, and more! Did I mention getting this style right first before moving on? Oh, I did? Well, that's because you just must!

Because you need the lines to stay the same throughout, and at the same thickness, you'll want to use a tool that will help you with that, like a pen. Stiff markers or pencils will work too.

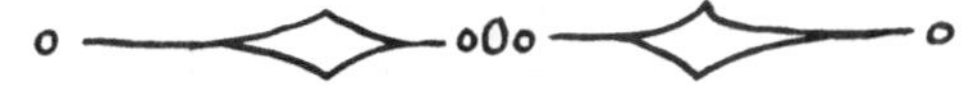

# TIME TO GET STARTED! ARE YOU READY?

Start by practicing the basic strokes below. Making sure your strokes are in the direction of the arrow and in number order. Keep the line consistent.

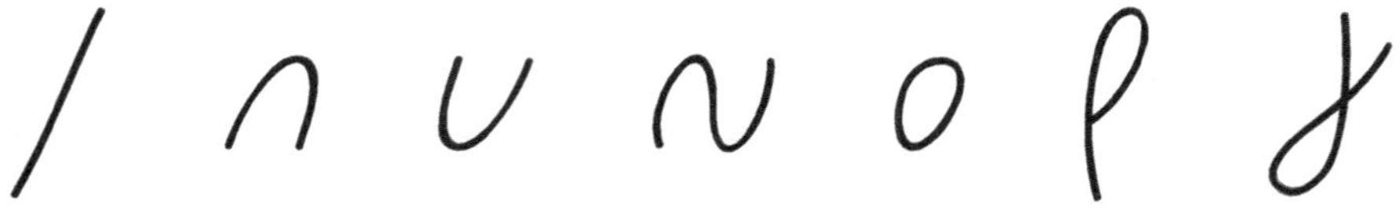

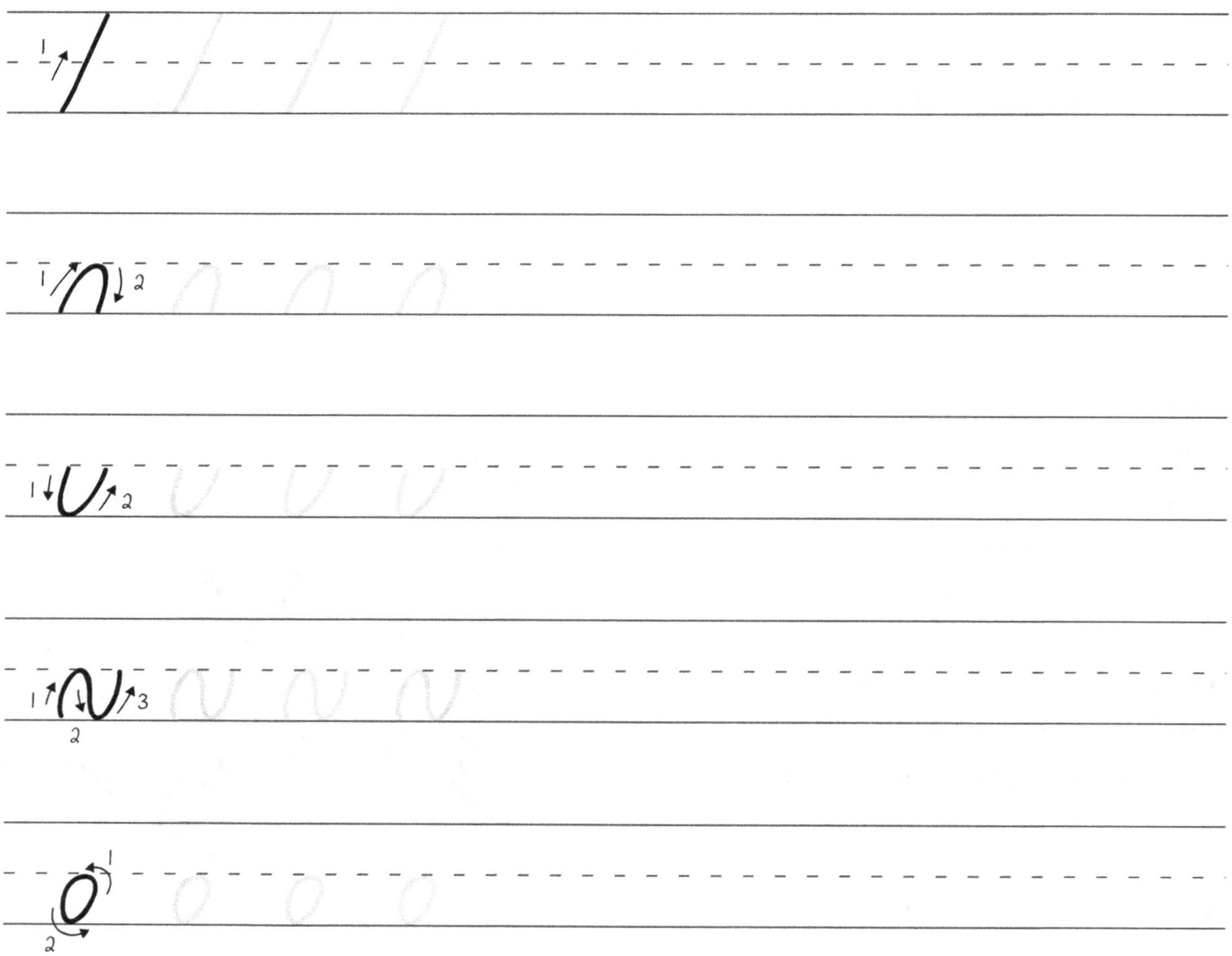

1

1 2

1 2

1 2 3

1 2

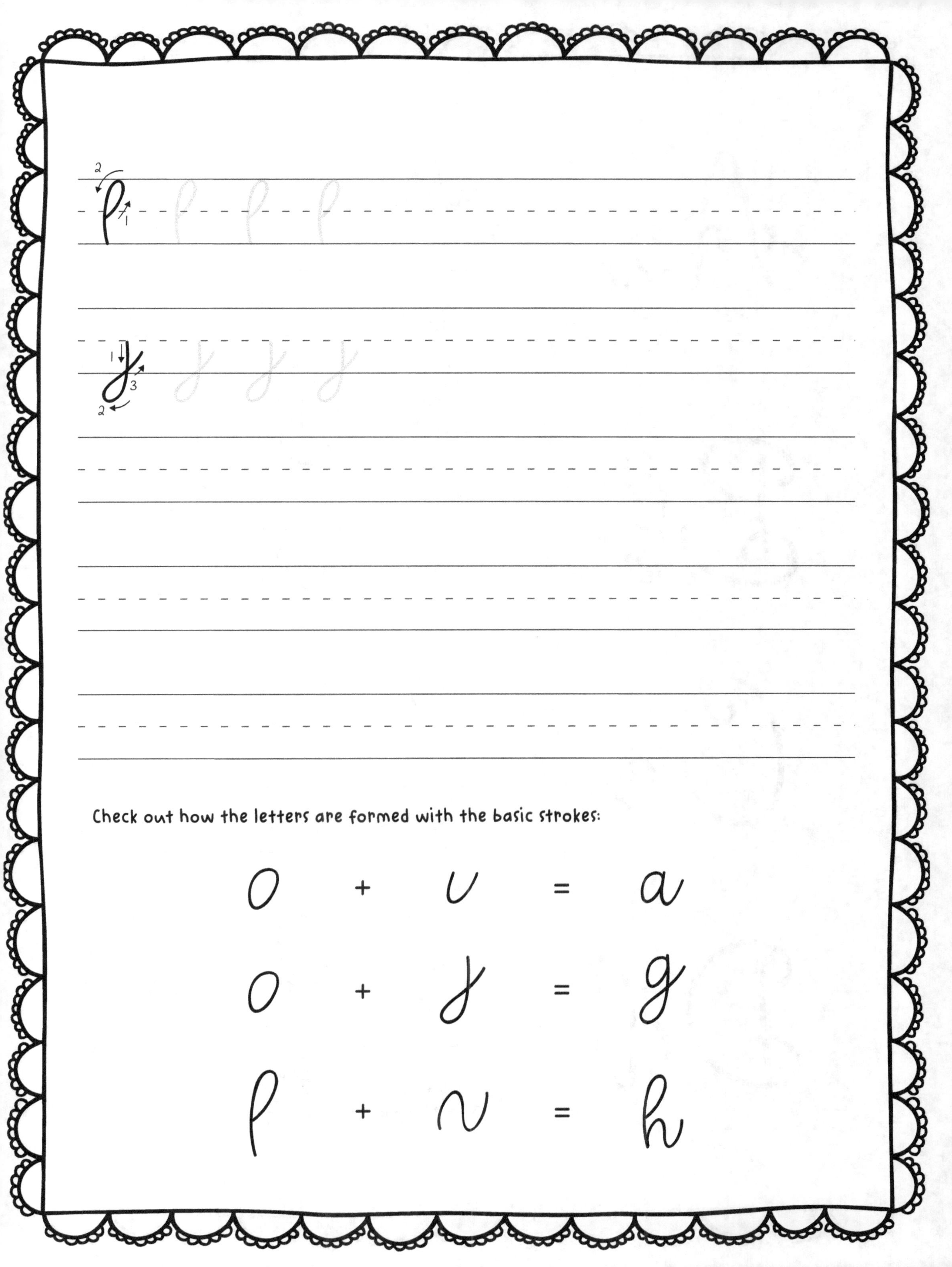
Check out how the letters are formed with the basic strokes:

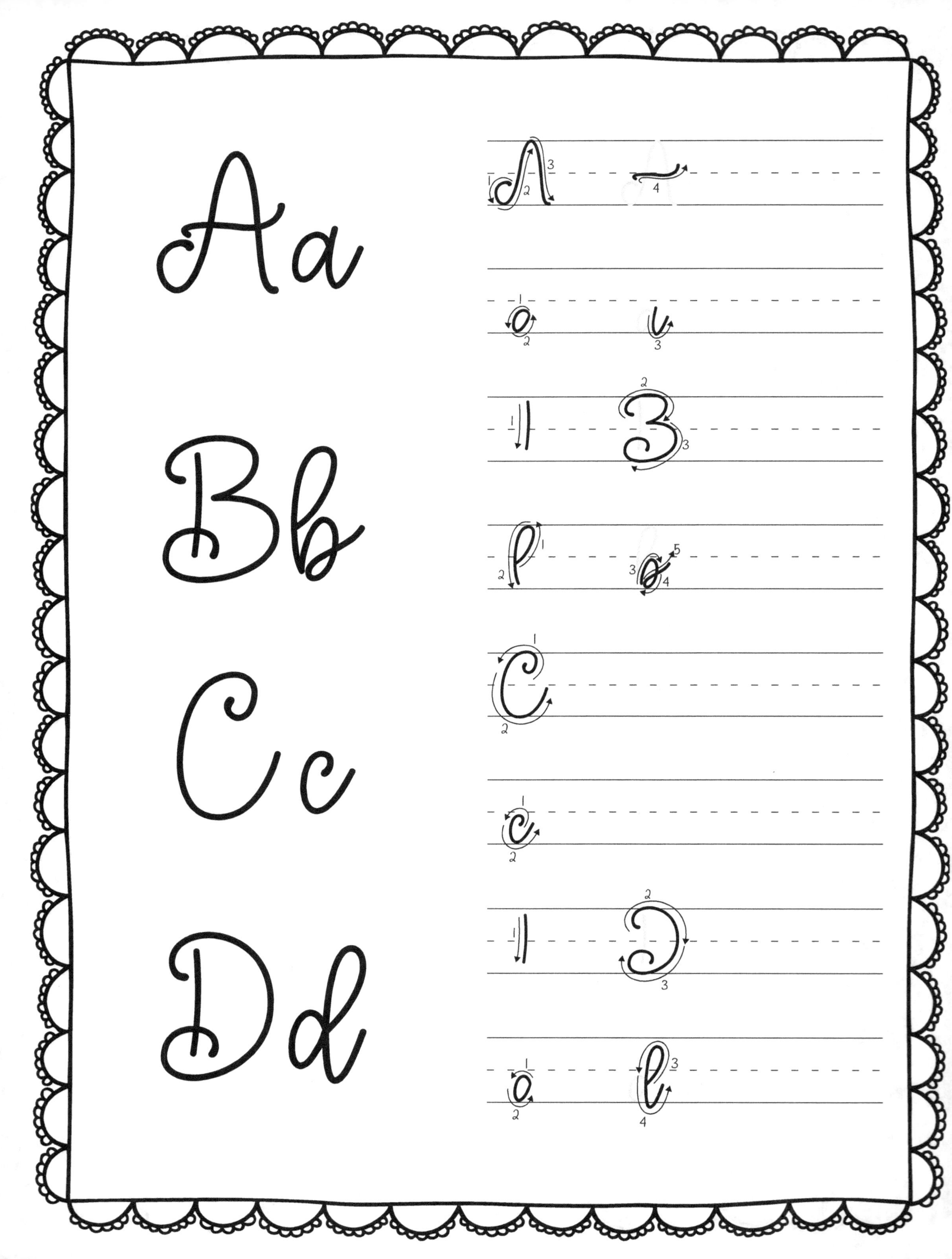

Aa
Bb
Cc
Dd

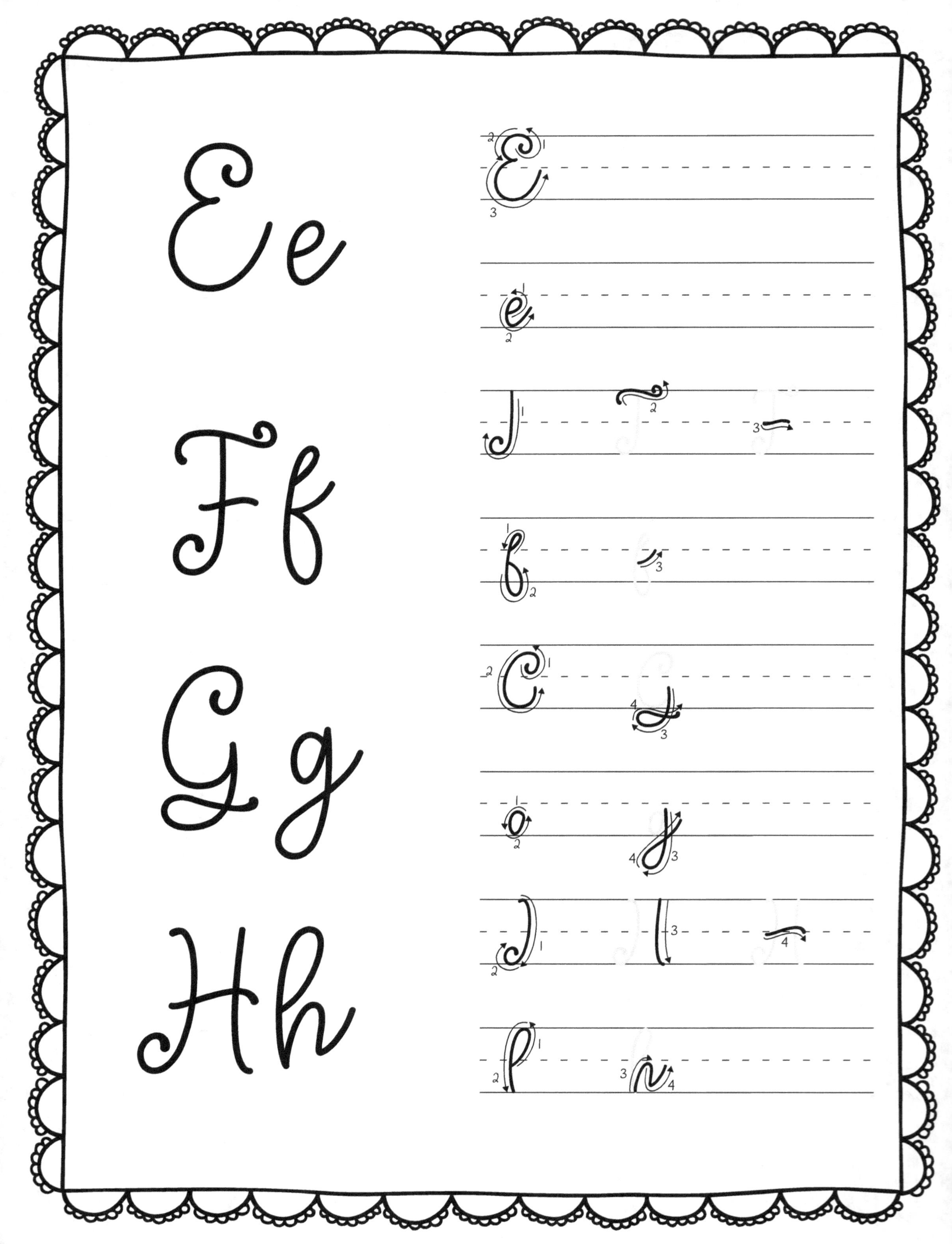

Ee
Ff
Gg
Hh

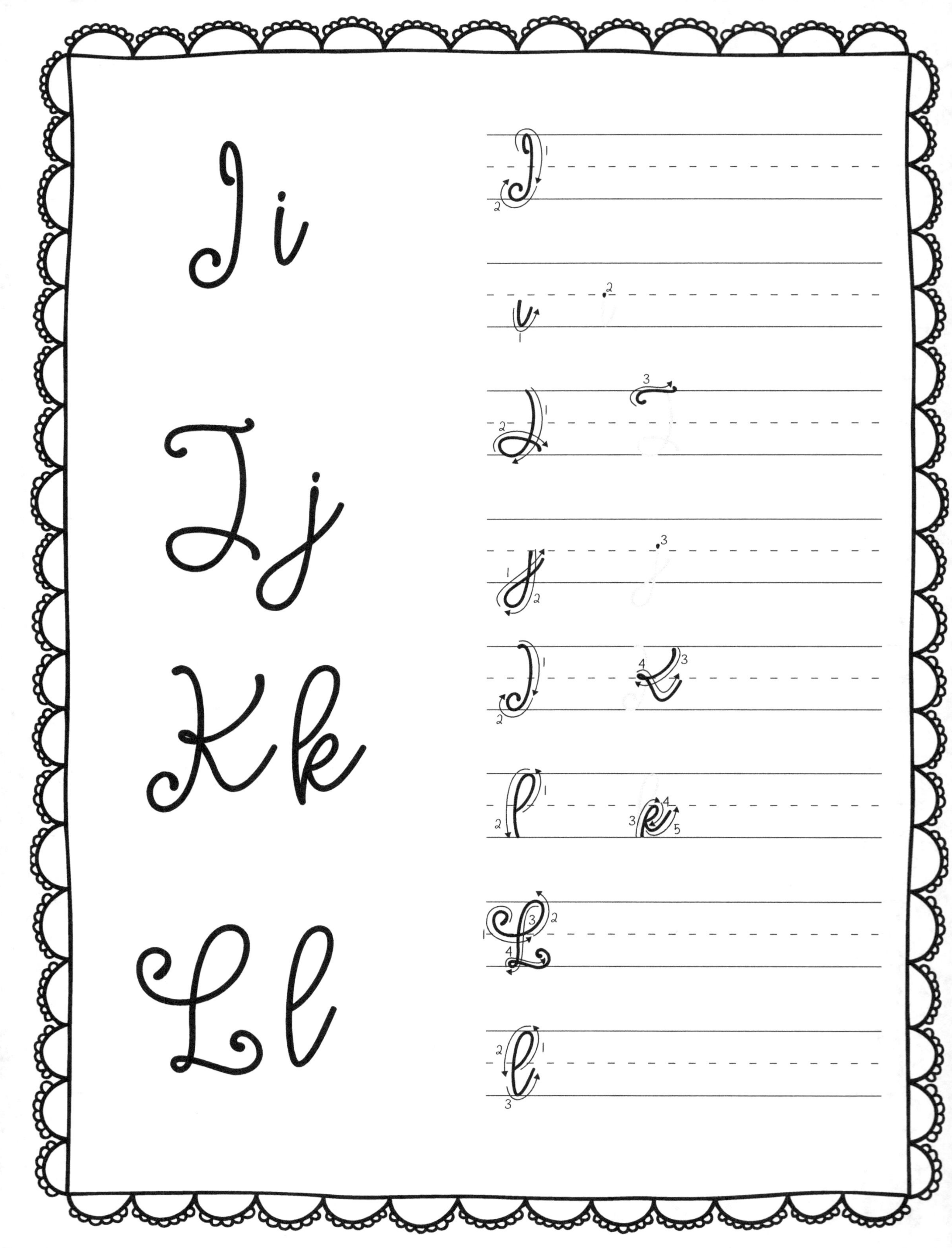

Ii
Jj
Kk
Ll

Monoline

Ii Ii Ii Ii Ii Ii Ii

Ii

Jj Jj Jj Jj Jj Jj

Jj

Kk Kk Kk Kk Kk Kk

Kk

Ll Ll Ll Ll Ll Ll

Ll

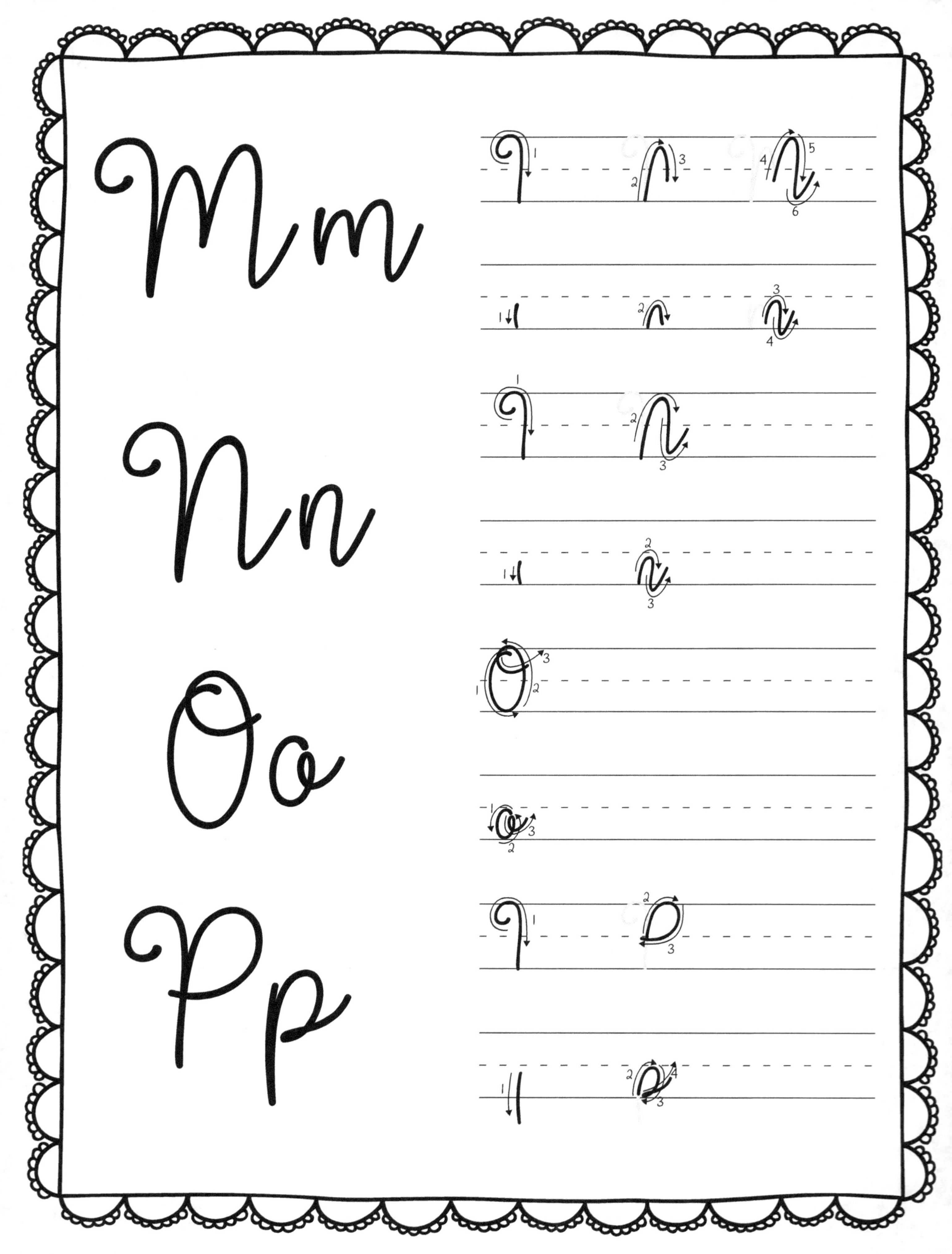
Mm
Nn
Oo
Pp

Mm Mm Mm Mm Mm Mm

Mm

Nn Nn Nn Nn Nn Nn

Nn

Oo Oo Oo Oo Oo Oo

Oo

Pp Pp Pp Pp Pp Pp

Pp

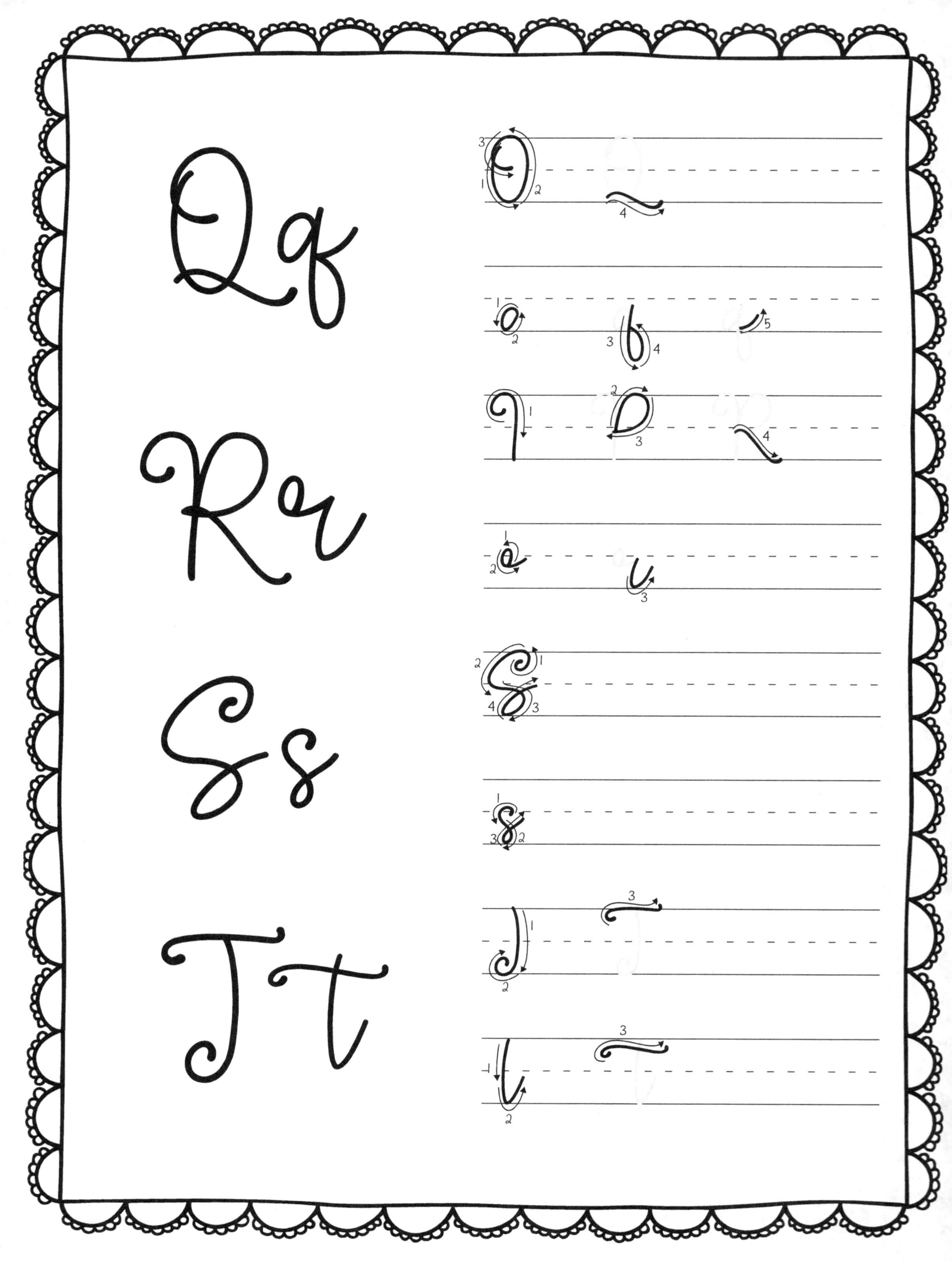
Qq
Rr
Ss
Tt

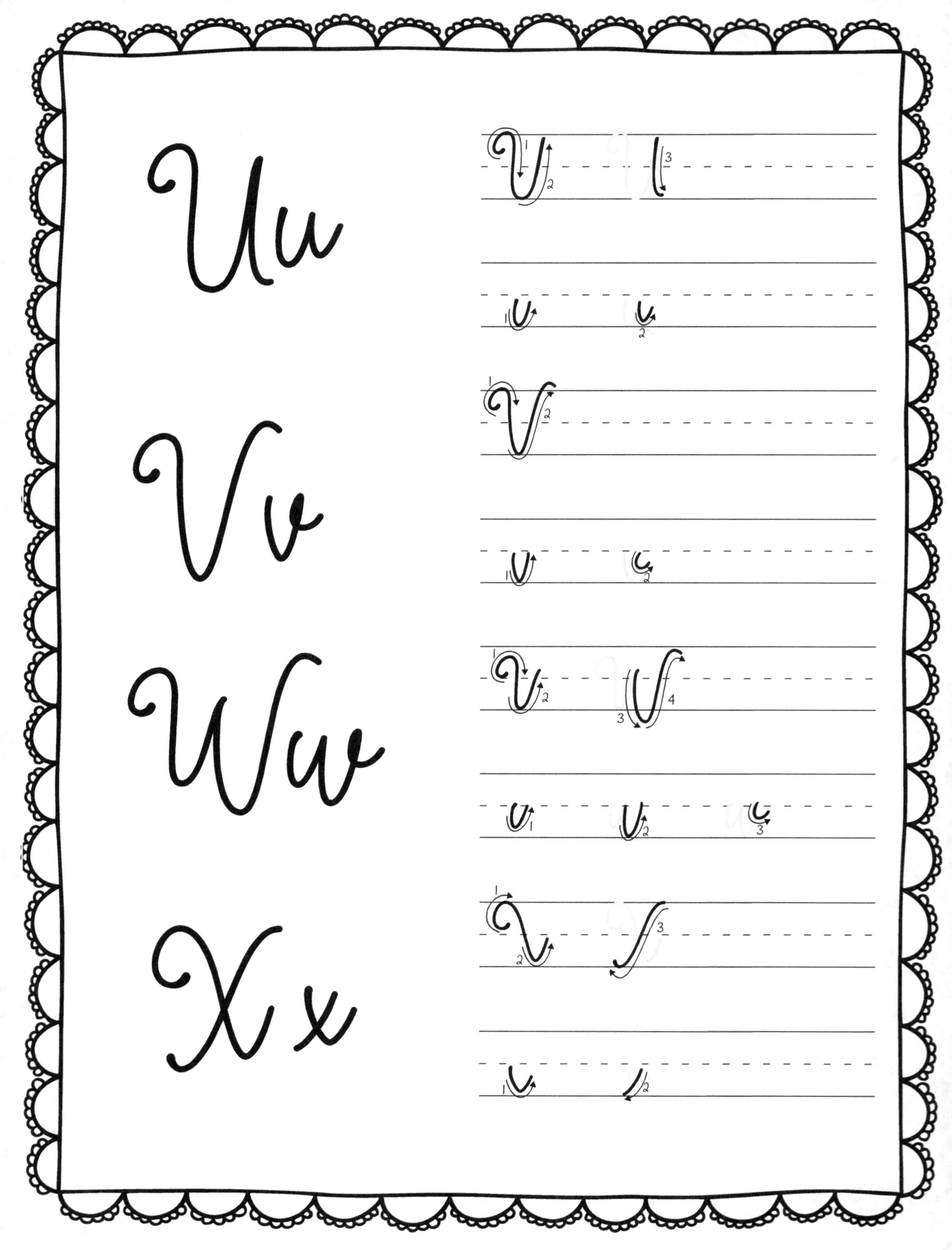
Uu
Vv
Ww
Xx

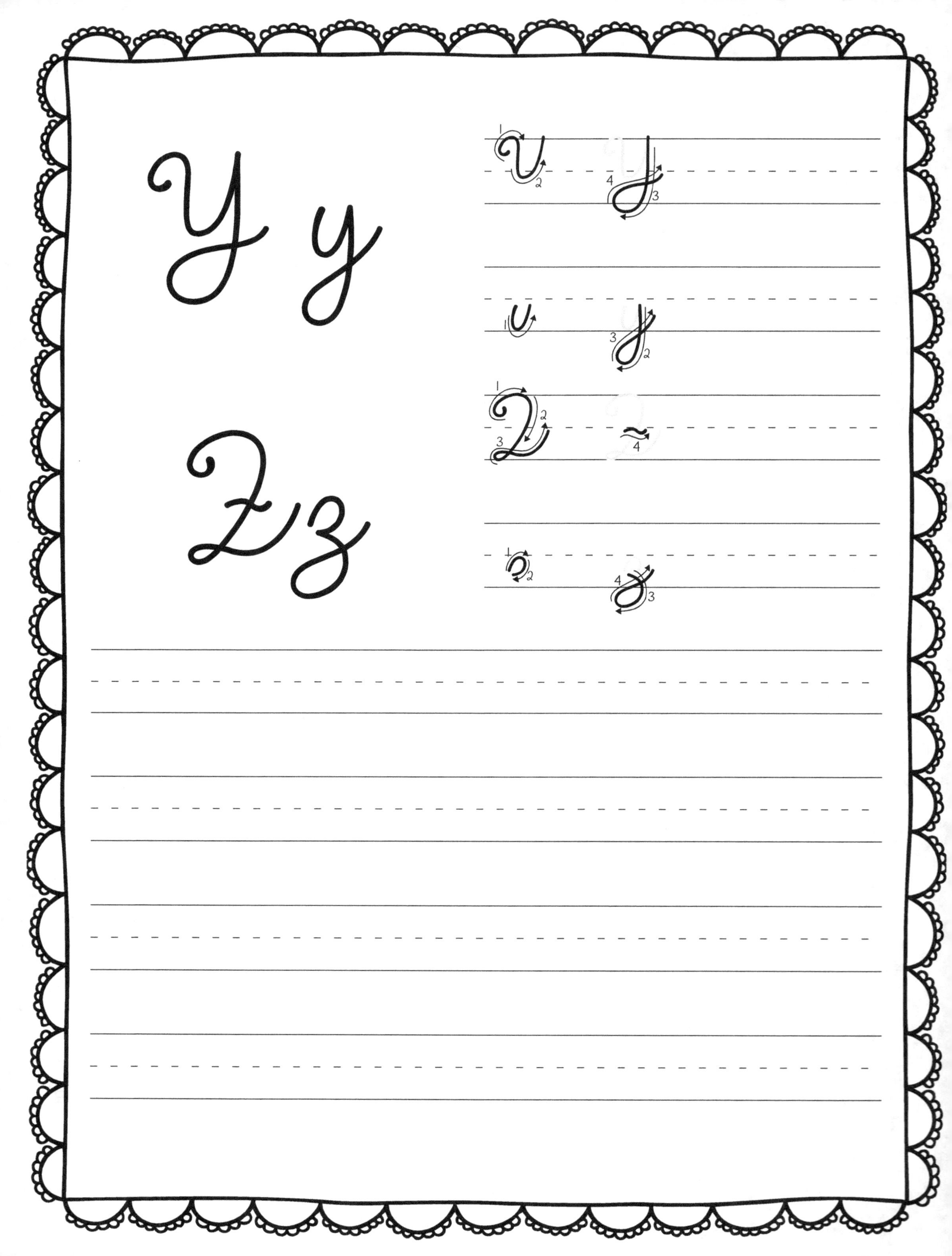

Yy
Zz

Yy Yy Yy Yy Yy Yy

Yy

Zz Zz Zz Zz Zz Zz

Zz

## Practice Again Here!

# Script Lettering Style

Aa Bb Cc Dd Ee

Ff Gg Hh Ii Jj

Kk Ll Mm Nn

Oo Pp Qq Rr Ss

Tt Uu Vv Ww

Xx Yy Zz

What do you think of this style? Pretty, hey? I think it's pretty Frenchie fancy, myself. At this point, you guys should be well-practiced in Monoline and ready to branch out into new styles. You're not? Well, go back to Monoline!

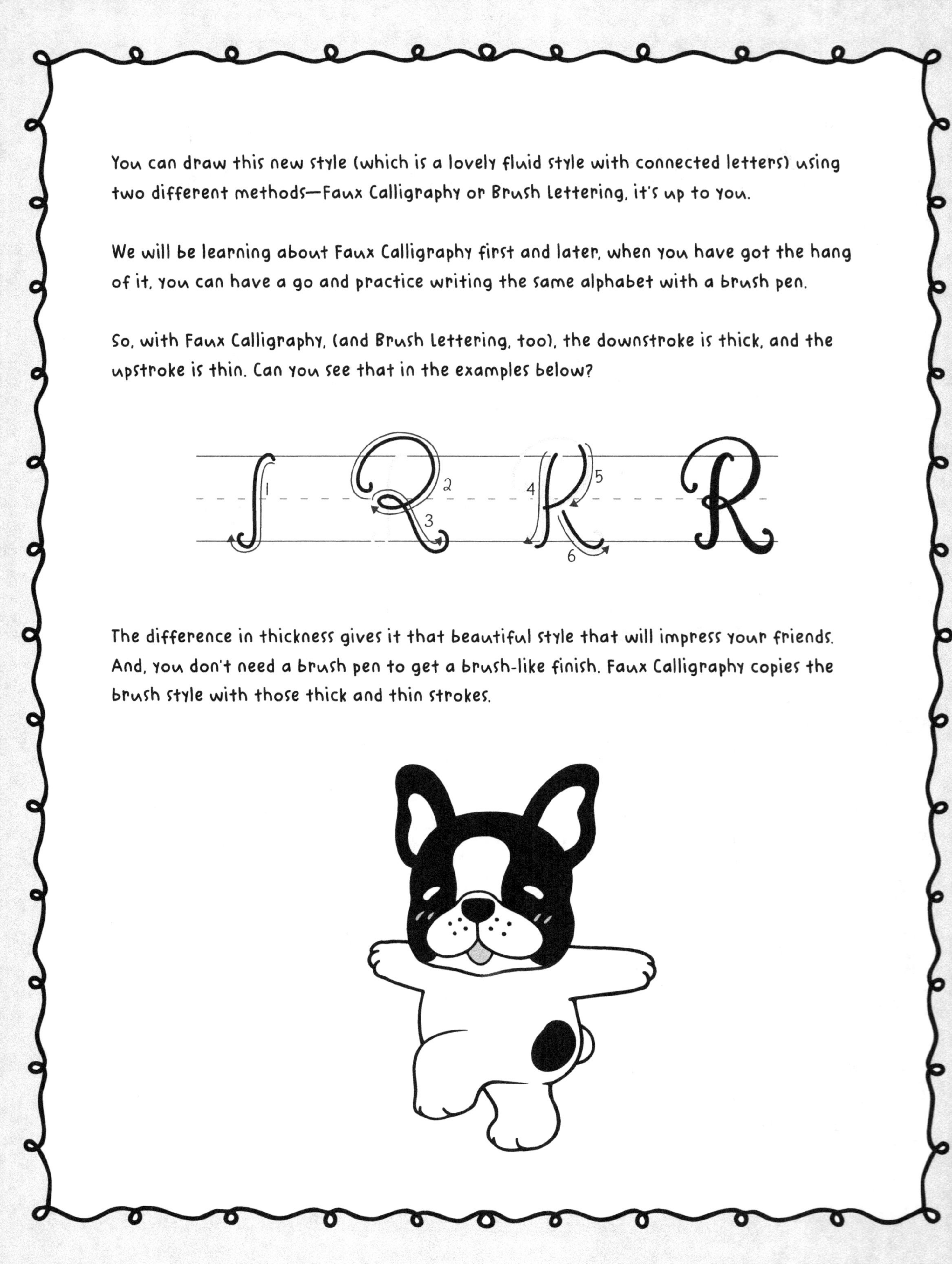

You can draw this new style (which is a lovely fluid style with connected letters) using two different methods—Faux Calligraphy or Brush Lettering, it's up to you.

We will be learning about Faux Calligraphy first and later, when you have got the hang of it, you can have a go and practice writing the same alphabet with a brush pen.

So, with Faux Calligraphy, (and Brush Lettering, too), the downstroke is thick, and the upstroke is thin. Can you see that in the examples below?

The difference in thickness gives it that beautiful style that will impress your friends. And, you don't need a brush pen to get a brush-like finish. Faux Calligraphy copies the brush style with those thick and thin strokes.

Have a go at these practice pages trying out the thicker downstroke. Follow the direction of the arrows, and those little numbers telling you the order of the strokes, and take your time!

Upstroke

Thicken the downstroke

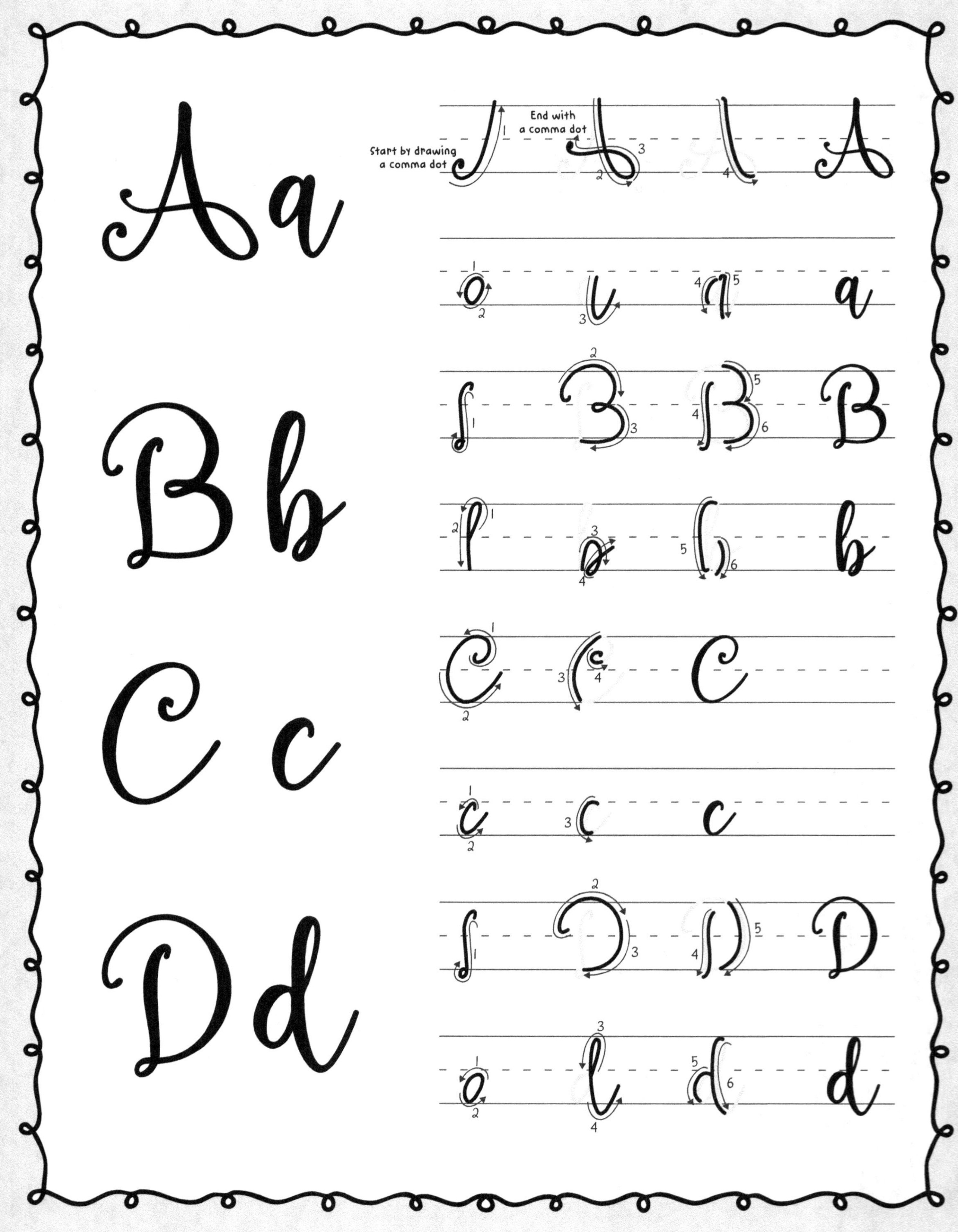
Aa
Bb
Cc
Dd
Start by drawing a comma dot
End with a comma dot

Aa Aa Aa Aa Aa Aa

Aa

Bb Bb Bb Bb Bb Bb

Bb

Cc Cc Cc Cc Cc Cc

Cc

Dd Dd Dd Dd Dd Dd

Dd

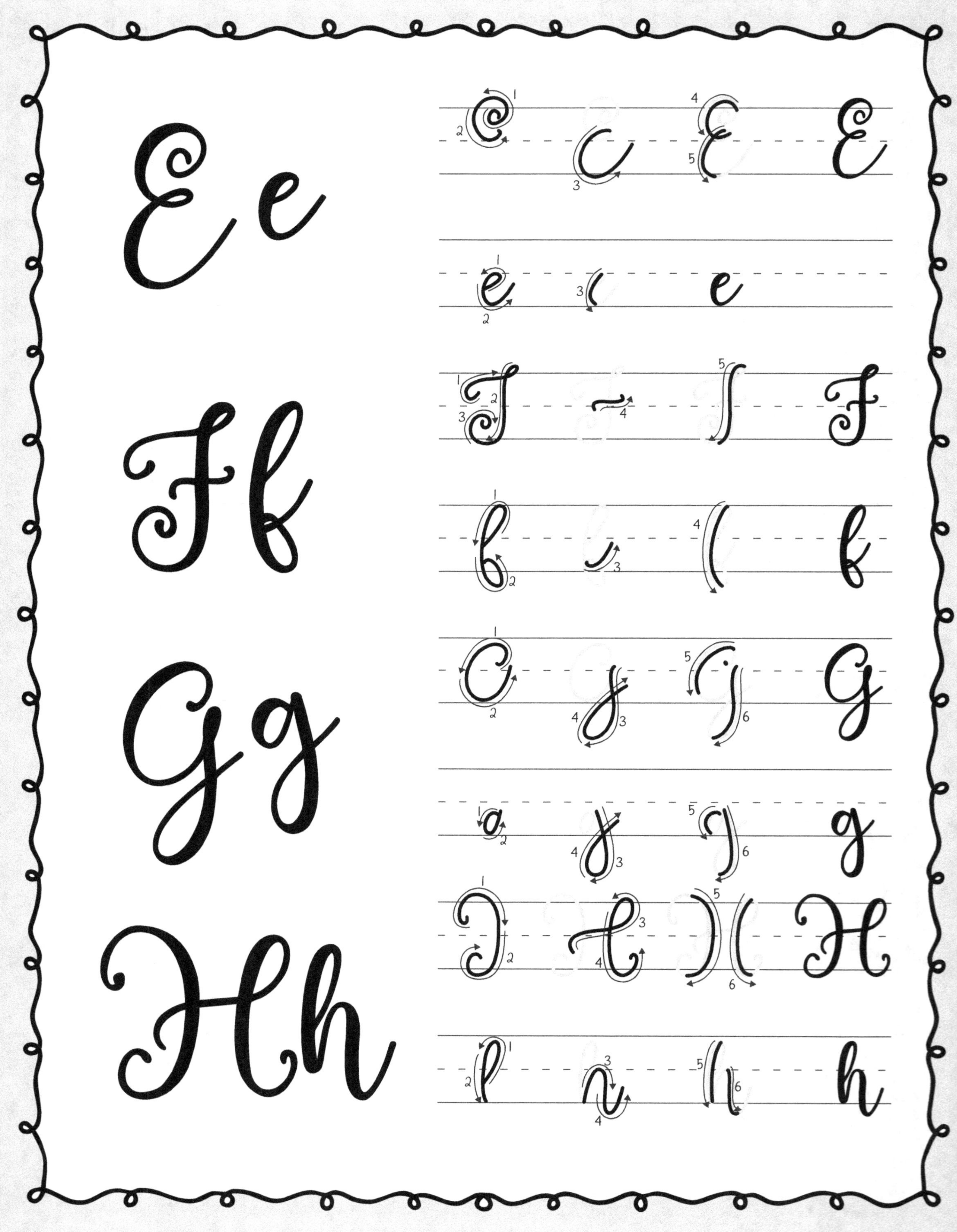

Ee Ee Ee Ee Ee Ee

Ee

Ff Ff Ff Ff Ff Ff

Ff

Gg Gg Gg Gg Gg Gg

Gg

Hh Hh Hh Hh Hh Hh

Hh

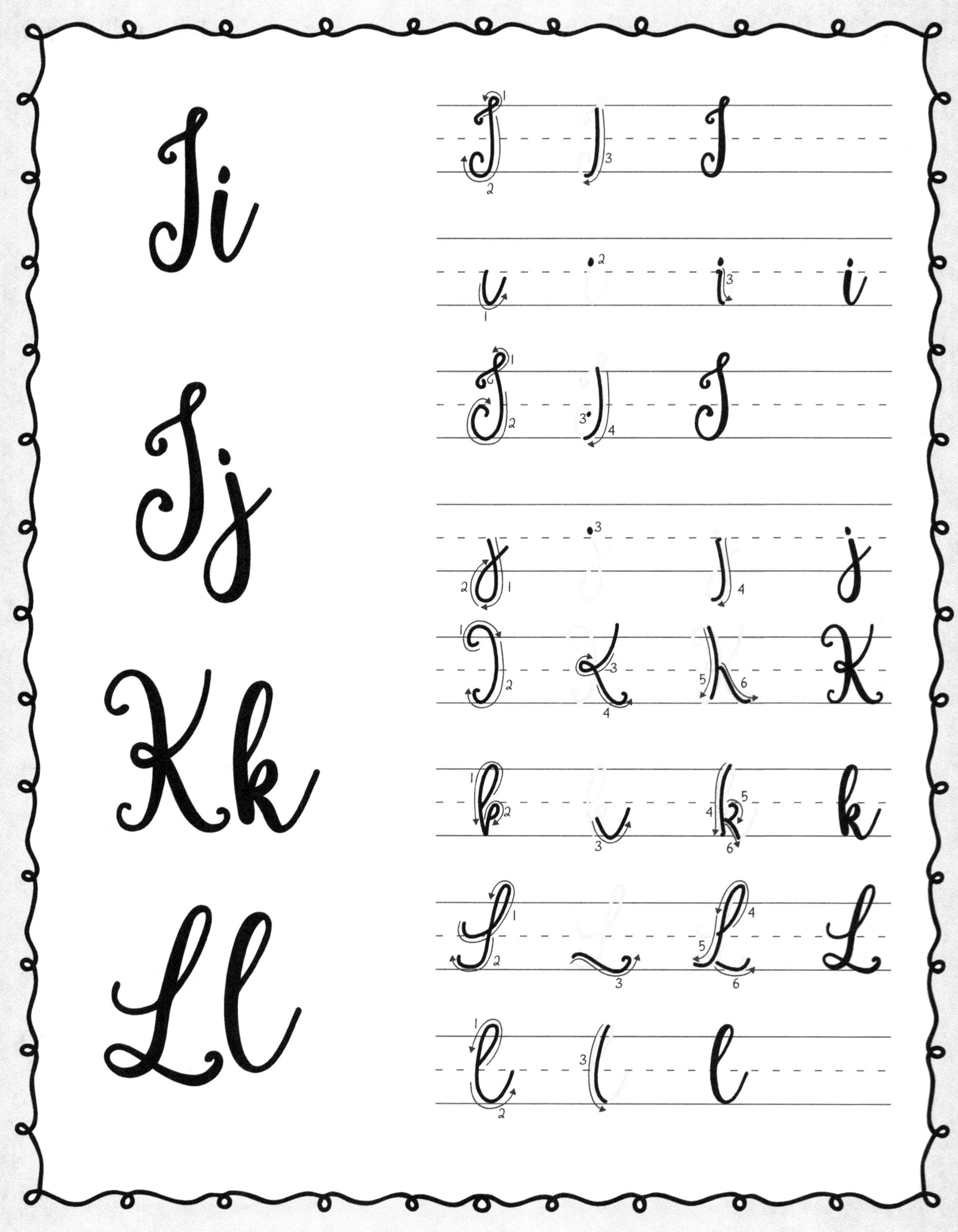

Ii Ii Ii Ii Ii Ii

Ii

Jj Jj Jj Jj Jj Jj

Jj

Kk Kk Kk Kk Kk Kk

Kk

Ll Ll Ll Ll Ll Ll

Ll

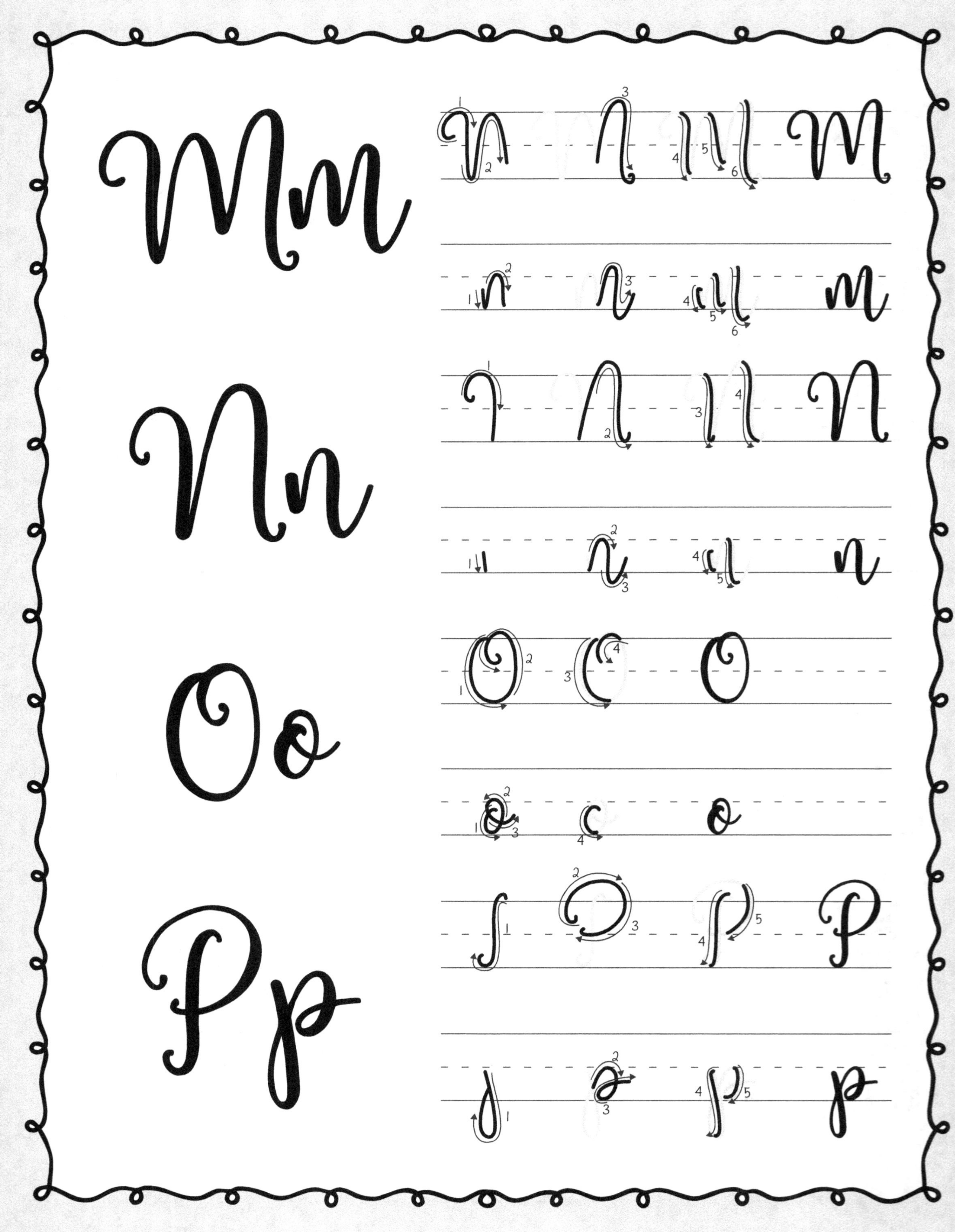

Mm
Nn
Oo
Pp

Mm Mm Mm Mm Mm

Mm

Nn Nn Nn Nn Nn Nn

Nn

Oo Oo Oo Oo Oo Oo

Oo

Pp Pp Pp Pp Pp Pp

Pp

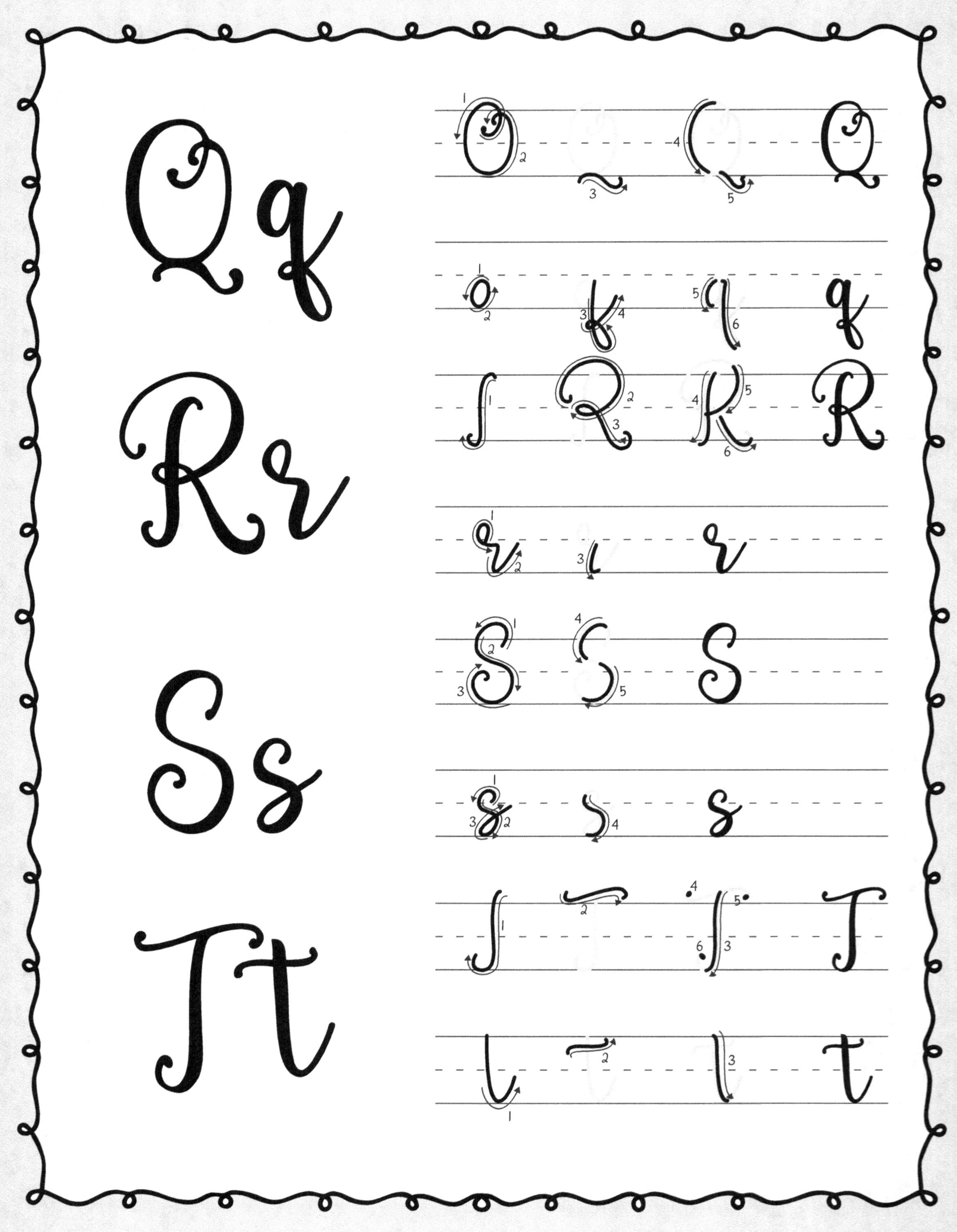

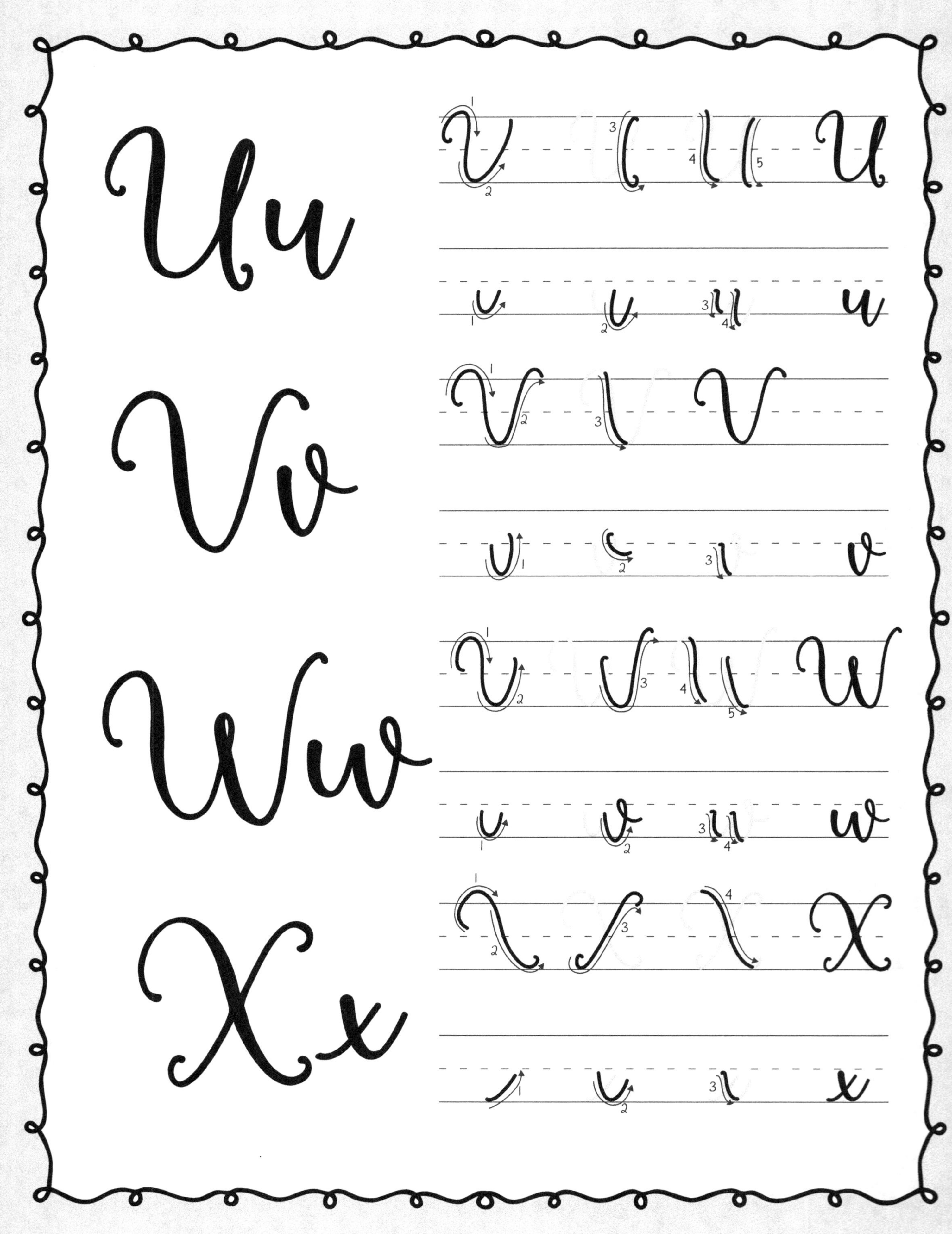

Uu
Vv
Ww
Xx

Uu Uu Uu Uu Uu Uu

Uu

Vv Vv Vv Vv Vv Vv

Vv

Ww Ww Ww Ww Ww

Ww

Xx Xx Xx Xx Xx Xx

Xx

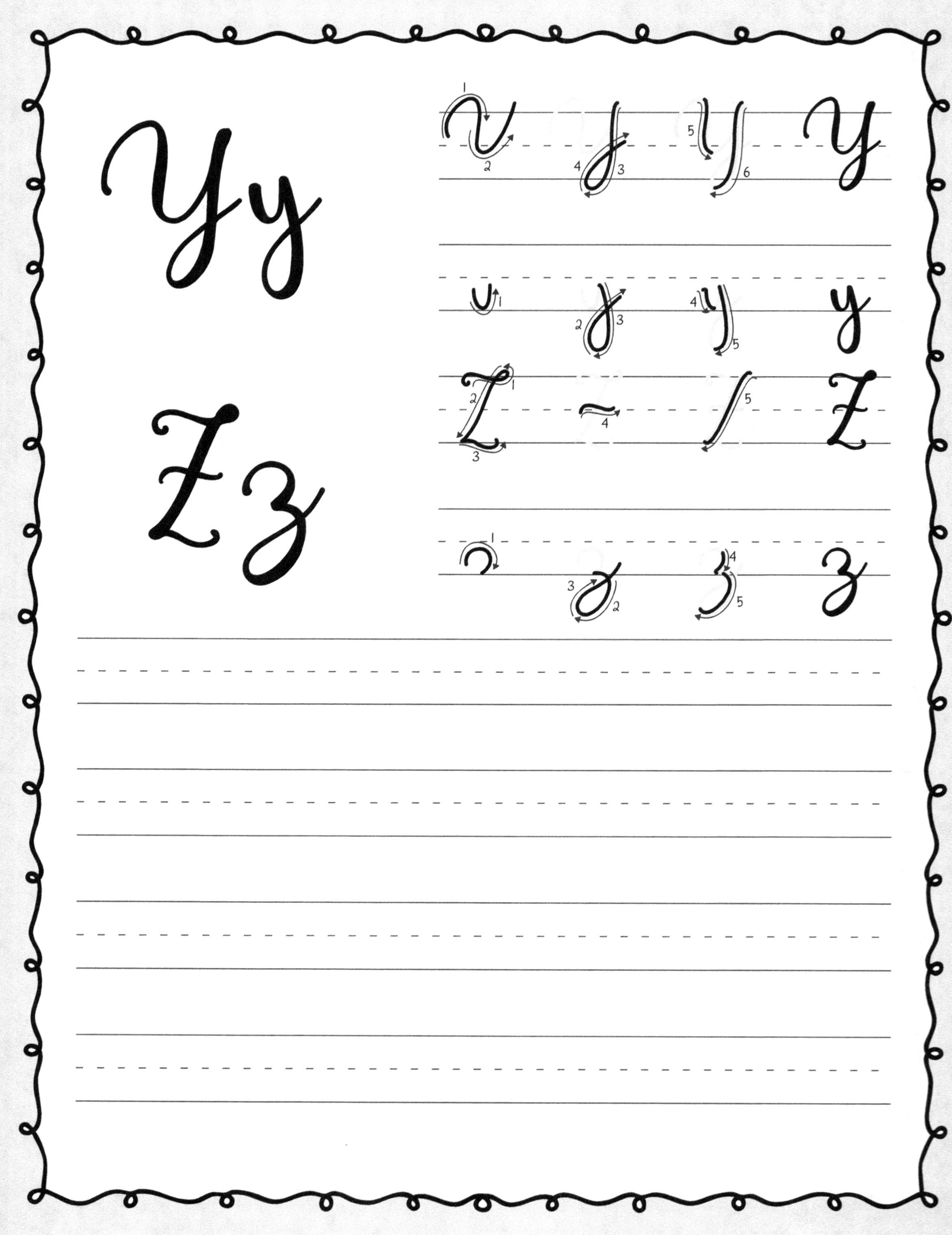

Yy
Zz

Yy Yy Yy Yy Yy Yy

Yy

Zz Zz Zz Zz Zz Zz

Zz

# NOW, HAVE A GO WITH A BRUSH PEN!

As I said, this is trickier (as brush pens are harder to control) but, I think, funner—is that a word? I don't think so! It will be 'more fun', I think!

You can try it out using different pressures and check out the results. Play while you practice. Once you get the knack of this, you can write lovely cards, and invitations-whatever you like.

## HERE ARE SOME TIPS:

- Go slow
- Pick up your pen after each stroke—to give you a better grip and more control over the brush pen.
- Keep your grip loose and relaxed—chill, guys!
- Practice
- Practice
- Practice

Like you did before, practice those basic strokes first. Then move on to the letters. Add pressure and push your brush pen down when you are making a down-stroke, this will create a thicker line. Have fun brush penning. Hang on, I don't think that's correct. Have fun with your brush pen!

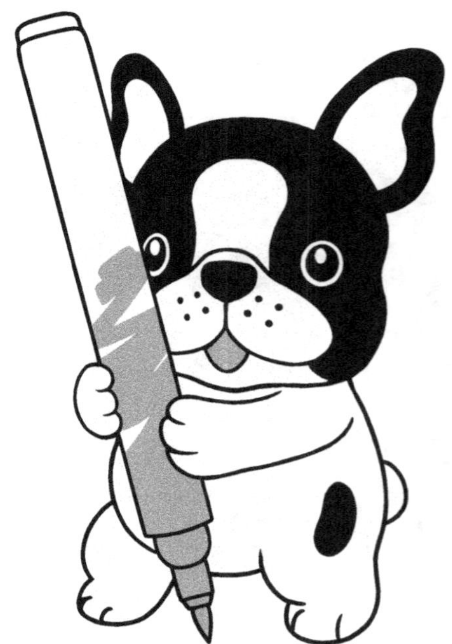

Do not add pressure to get a nice, thin line.

Press down harder to get a thick line.

Go slow with this one! Start with a nice, curved upstroke and add pressure half way.

This time begin with a thick downstroke and release pressure halfway.

Oh, this is a tricky one! There are three parts to this stroke. Start with a thin upstroke. then add pressure to draw a thick downstroke, repeat an upstroke again.

To form an oval: Start with a light upstroke (to the right, at around 1 o'clock) and curve anticlockwise. At the bottom, release pressure and draw a curved upstroke.

Start at the mean line and form an oval-like shape.
Keep the pen moving and finish the loop with a thick downstroke.

This time, start with a thick downstroke and release pressure to curve back up.

Now it's time to practice the letters. Remember, thin upstroke and thick downstroke.

a a a a a a a a a a

a a a

b b b b b b b b b b

b b b

c c c c c c c c c c

c c c

d d d d d d d d d d

d d d

i

3 1 2

j

4 1 3 2

k

2 1 3 4

l

2 1 3

u u u u u u u u u u
u u u

v v v v v v v v v v
v v v

w w w w w w w w w w
w w w

x x x x x x x x x x
x x x

y 1 2 3 4 5

z 1 2 3 4 5

A

B

C

D

M

N

O

P

Y

1 2 3 4 5

Z

1 2 3 4 5

## Practice Again Here!

# Sans Serif & Serif

As mentioned earlier, Sans Serif is a more modern style that doesn't have any little added bits to the ends of the letters while Serif does.

I wonder, which one do you prefer?

Sans Serif may not have those extra little bits, but it's still super fun to do. You can vary the size and the width of the letters and have a really good play around. The style is neat and fresh, will go well with other more decorative details in your artwork, and so it's a very handy skill to have. You can use any type of tool for Sans Serif, as long as it gives nice consistent lines. Try pens, markers, colored pencils, or crayons.

Below, Sans Serif is on the left and Serif is on the right.

## Sans Serif

Aa Bb Cc Dd
Ee Ff Gg Hh
Ii Jj Kk Ll
Mm Nn Oo Pp
Qq Rr Ss Tt
Uu Vv Ww Xx
Yy Zz

## Serif

Aa Bb Cc Dd
Ee Ff Gg Hh
Ii Jj Kk Ll
Mm Nn Oo Pp
Qq Rr Ss Tt
Uu Vv Ww Xx
Yy Zz

Aa

Bb

Cc

Dd

| Sans Serif | Make it Serif! |
| --- | --- |
| A | A |
| a | a |
| B | B |
| b | b |
| C | C |
| c | c |
| D | D |
| d | d |

Sans Serif

Try adding Serif!

Aa Aa Aa

Aa

Bb Bb Bb

Bb

Cc Cc Cc

Cc

Dd Dd Dd

Dd

Aa Aa Aa

Aa

Bb Bb Bb

Bb

Cc Cc Cc

Cc

Dd Dd Dd

Dd

Ee

Ff

Gg

Hh

| Sans Serif | Make it Serif! |
|---|---|
| E: 1 2 3 4 | 5 6 E |
| e: 1 2 3 | 4 e |
| F: 1 2 3 | 4 5 F |
| f: 1 2 | 3 f |
| G: 1 2 3 4 | 5 G |
| g: 1 2 3 | 4 5 g |
| H: 1 2 3 | 4 5 H |
| h: 1 2 | 3 4 5 h |

Sans Serif

Try adding Serif!

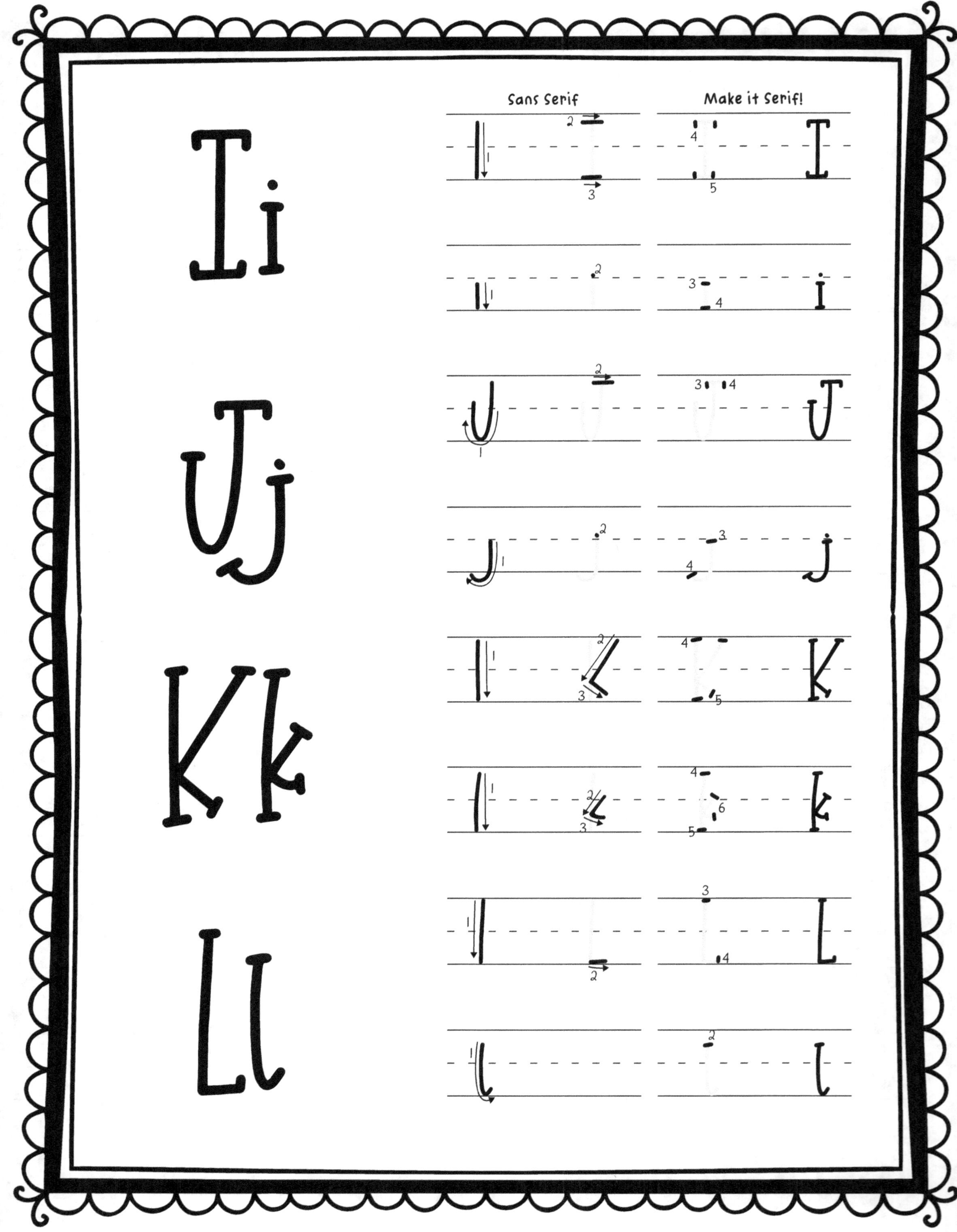

Ii
Jj
Kk
Ll
Sans Serif
Make it Serif!

Sans Serif

Try adding Serif!

Ii Ii Ii | Ii Ii Ii

Ii | Ii

Jj Jj Jj | Jj Jj Jj

Jj | Jj

Kk Kk Kk | Kk Kk Kk

Kk | Kk

Ll Ll Ll | Ll Ll Ll

Ll | Ll

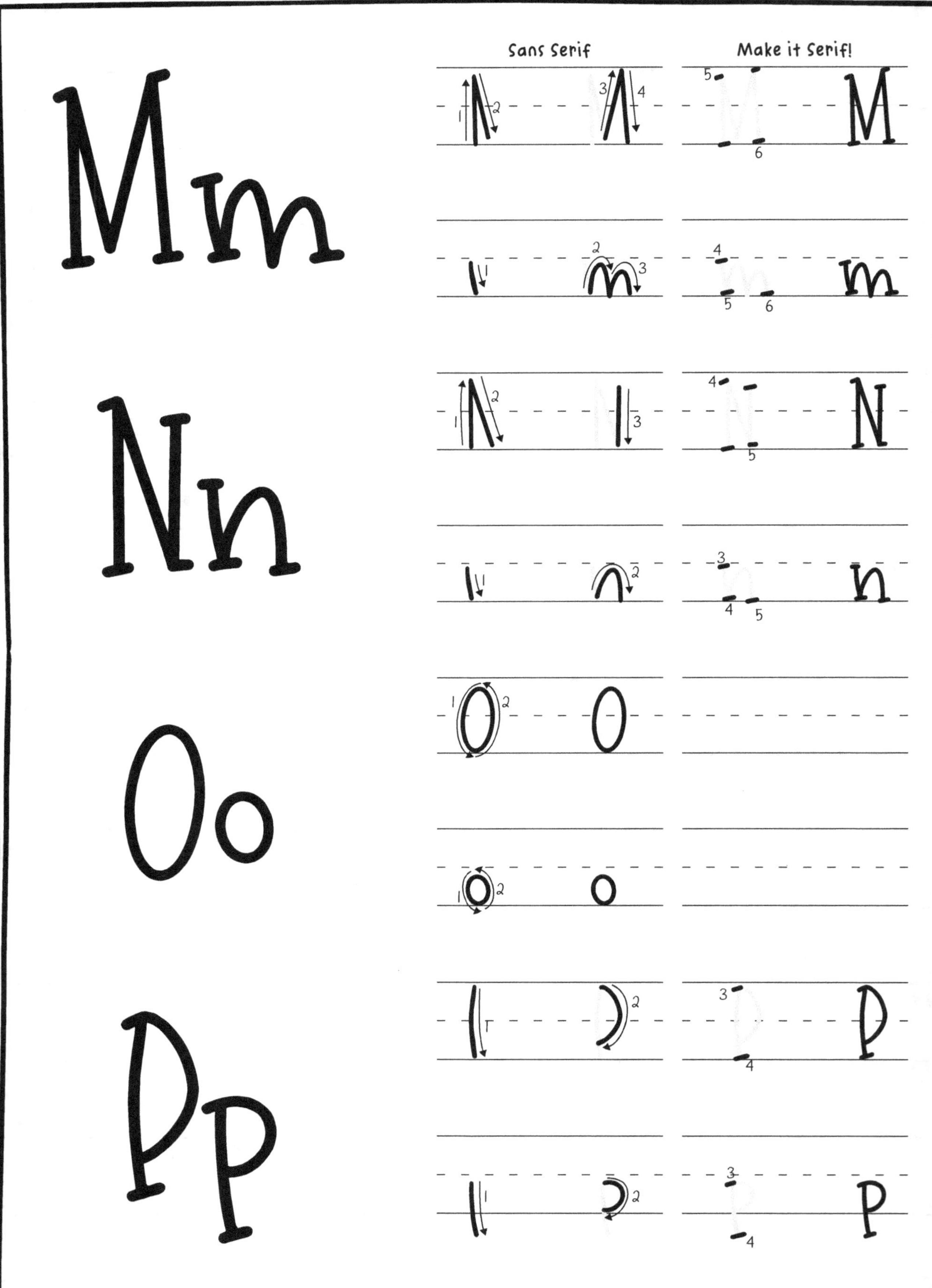

Mm
Nn
Oo
Pp
Sans Serif
Make it Serif!

| Sans Serif | Try adding Serif! |
| --- | --- |
| Mm Mm Mm | Mm Mm Mm |
| Mm | Mm |
| Nn Nn Nn | Nn Nn Nn |
| Nn | Nn |
| Oo Oo Oo | Oo Oo Oo |
| Oo | Oo |
| Pp Pp Pp | Pp Pp Pp |
| Pp | Pp |

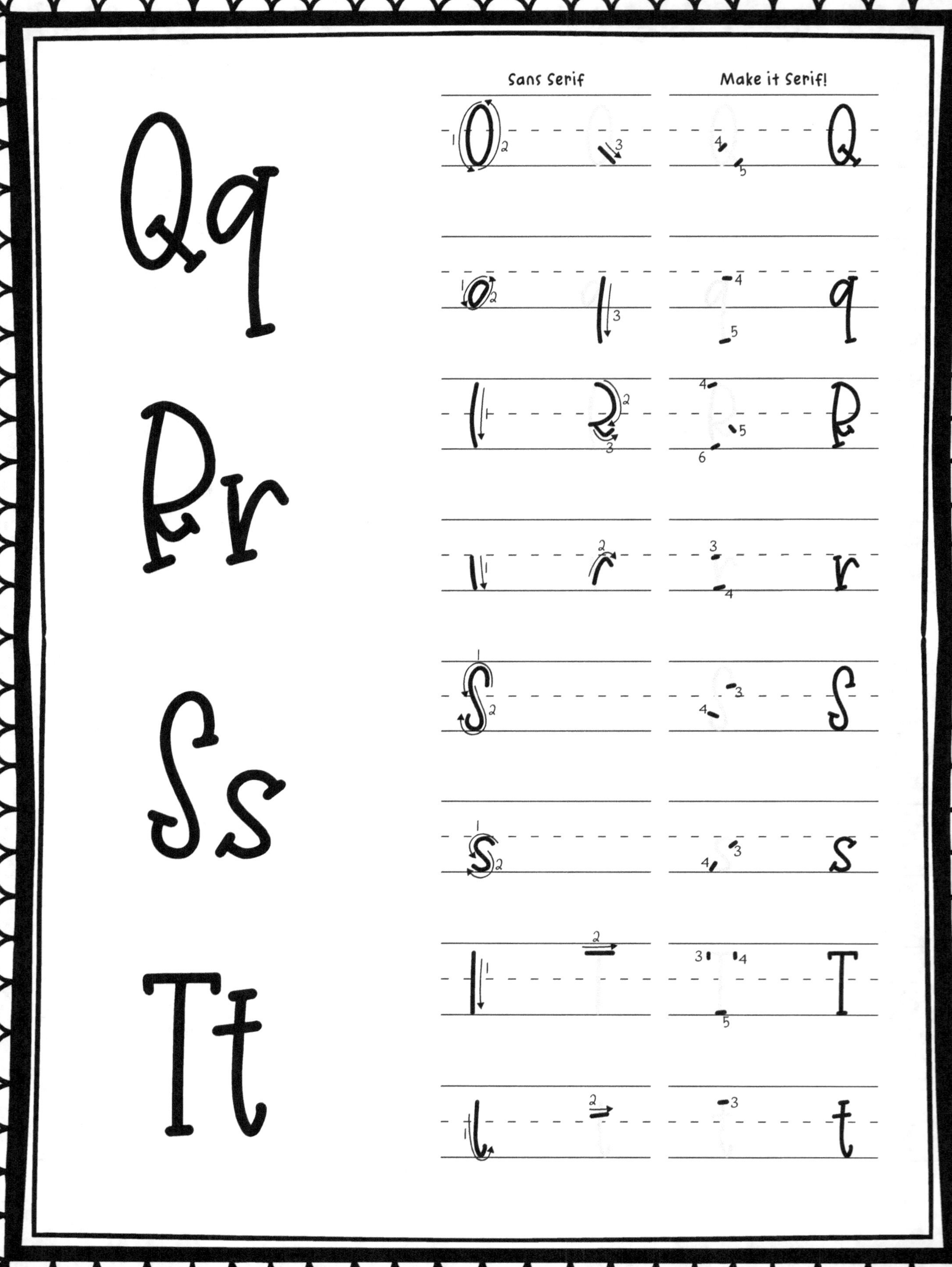

Qq
Rr
Ss
Tt
Sans Serif
Make it Serif!

Sans Serif

Try adding Serif!

Uu

Vv

Ww

Xx

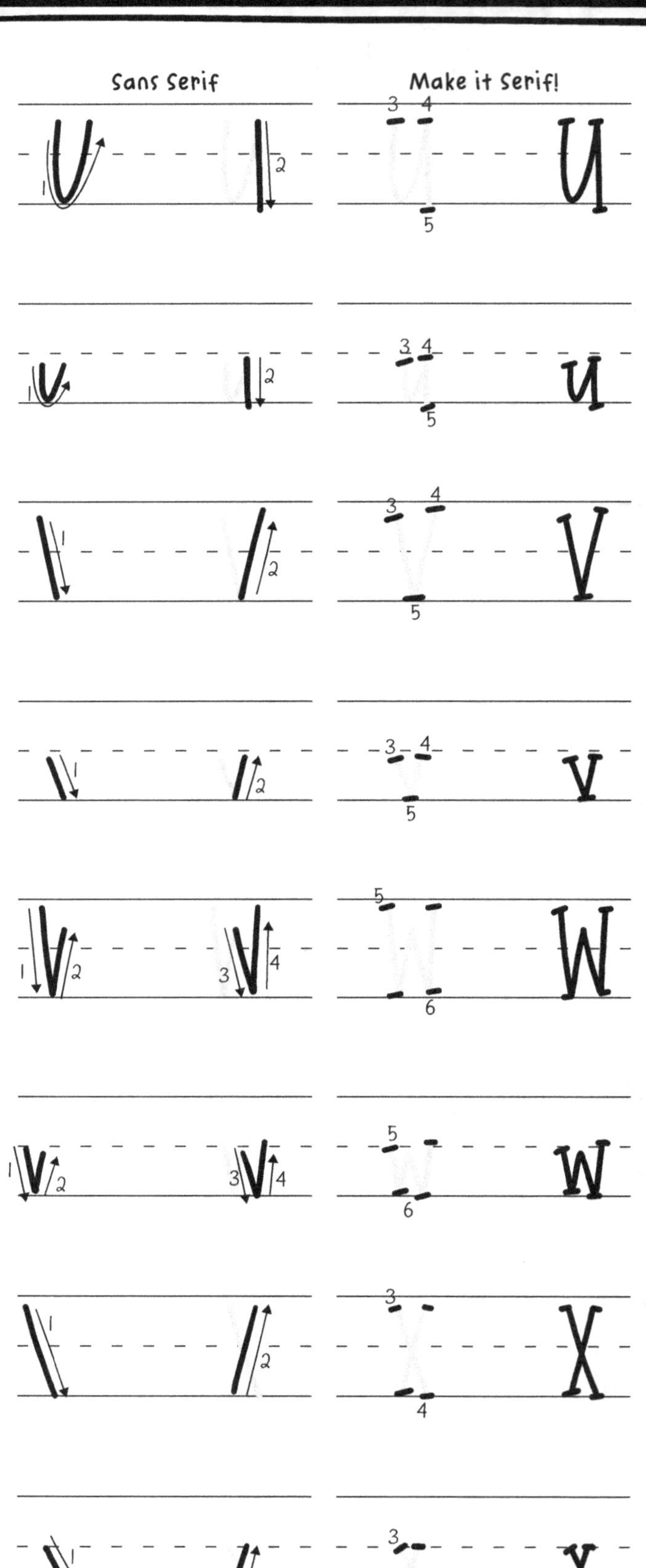

Sans Serif

Try adding Serif!

Uu Uu Uu

Uu

Uu Uu Uu

Uu

Vv Vv Vv

Vv

Vv Vv Vv

Vv

Ww Ww Ww

Ww

Ww Ww Ww

Ww

Xx Xx Xx

Xx

Xx Xx Xx

Xx

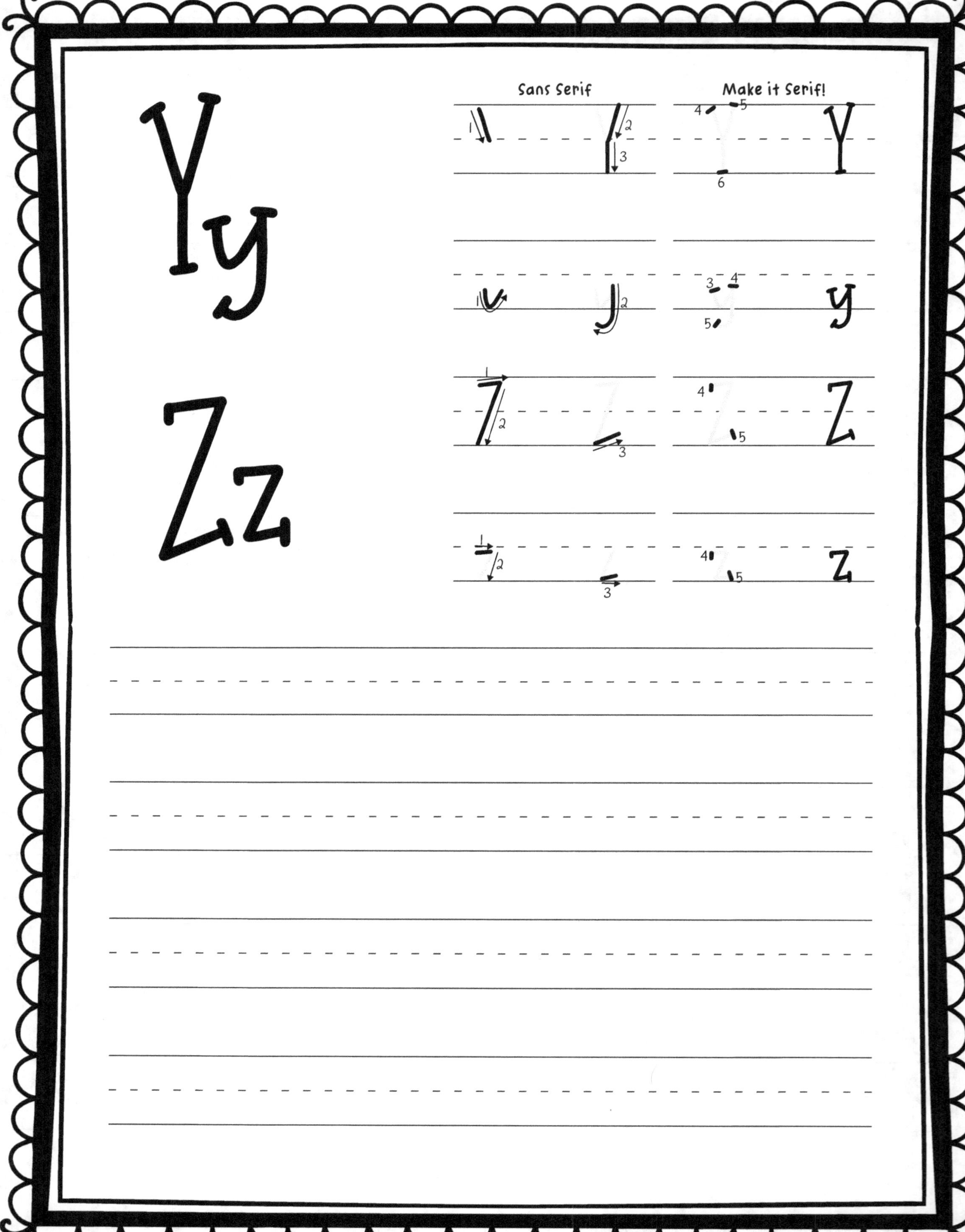

Yy
Zz
Sans Serif
Make it Serif!

Sans Serif

Try adding Serif!

Yy Yy Yy

Yy Yy Yy

Yy

Yy

Zz Zz Zz

Zz Zz Zz

Zz

Zz

## Practice Again Here!

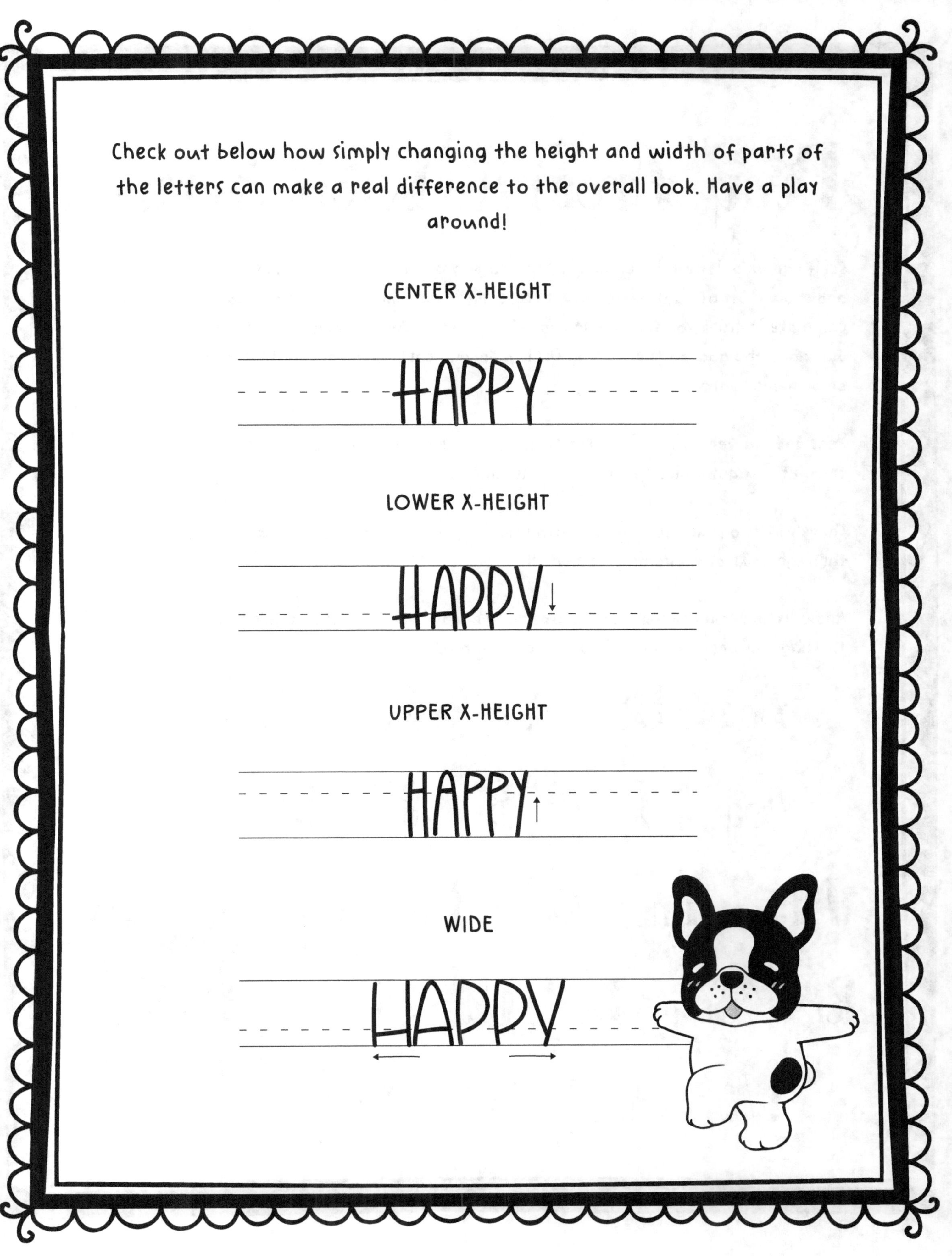

Check out below how simply changing the height and width of parts of the letters can make a real difference to the overall look. Have a play around!

CENTER X-HEIGHT

HAPPY

LOWER X-HEIGHT

HAPPY

UPPER X-HEIGHT

HAPPY

WIDE

HAPPY

# Play Around With Serif!

Serif can be a little trickier, but it's fun to play around with the endings of the letters and show a bit of your personality here. Serif is seen more as a traditional style, but you can make it quirky or flowing. It's totally up to you. Keep in mind the theme of your work and the goal of the writing—is it a formal card, or a cool font? Is it for a wedding or a themed party?

Pens and markers work great for Serif. Experiment with different tools, but choose ones that let you get a nice, clear, and precise line.

There's just so much you can do with Serif, so play around and see what flows down through your arm and onto the page!

And a little reminder here: make sure you've mastered the other styles first before tackling this one—it'll make it a lot easier for you.

Aa Bb Cc Dd Ee Ff

Gg Hh Ii Jj Kk Ll

Mm Nn Oo Pp Qq

Rr Ss Tt Uu Vv

Ww Xx Yy Zz

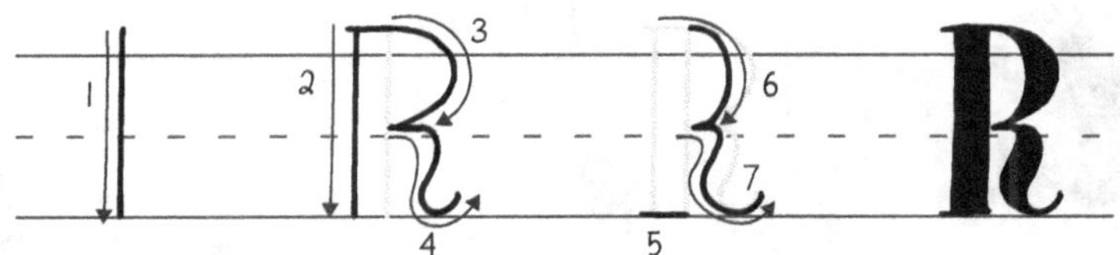


When starting to write Serif, begin your letter in Sans Serif and get a nice clean monoline look.

Next, add some extra weight to the bottom of the letter and add some extra downstrokes as you did in the Faux Calligraphy to give it some depth (in other words, make it look cool).

Lastly, fill in the letter and voila—you have written a letter in Serif!

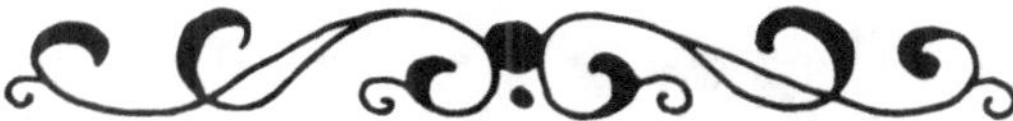

You can also have fun decorating the blank spaces—anything goes! And what a difference a few dots and lines make.

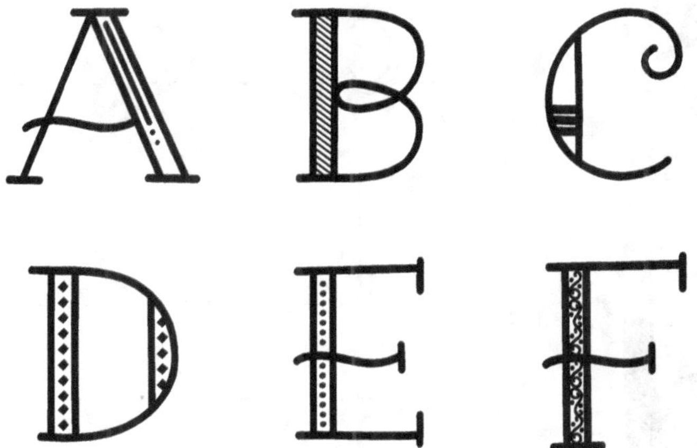

Aa

Bb

Cc

Dd

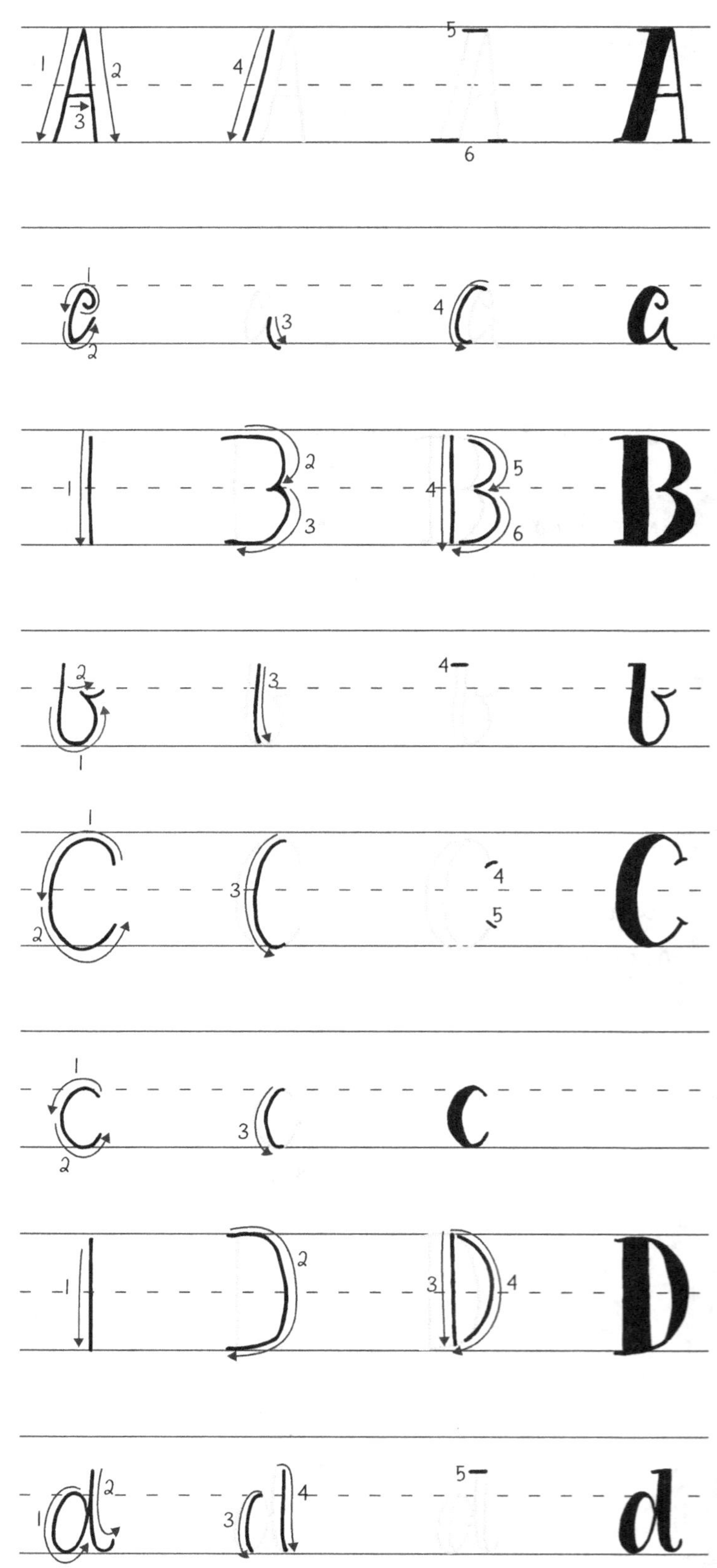

Aa Aa Aa Aa Aa Aa

Aa

Bb Bb Bb Bb Bb Bb

Bb

Cc Cc Cc Cc Cc Cc

Cc

Dd Dd Dd Dd Dd Dd

Dd

Ee

Ff

Gg

Hh

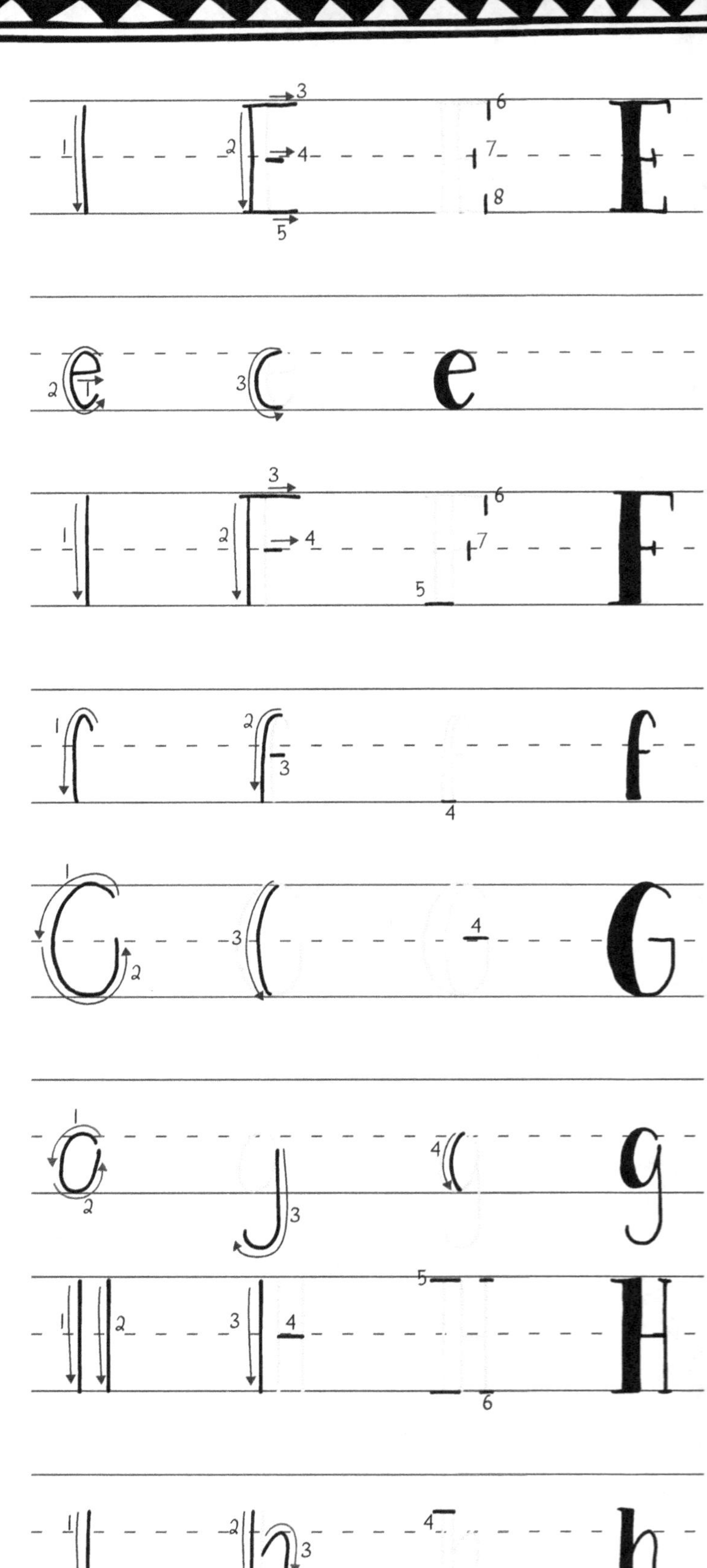

Ee Ee Ee Ee Ee Ee

Ee

Ff Ff Ff Ff Ff Ff

Ff

Gg Gg Gg Gg Gg Gg

Gg

Hh Hh Hh Hh Hh Hh

Hh

Ii

Jj

Kk

Ll

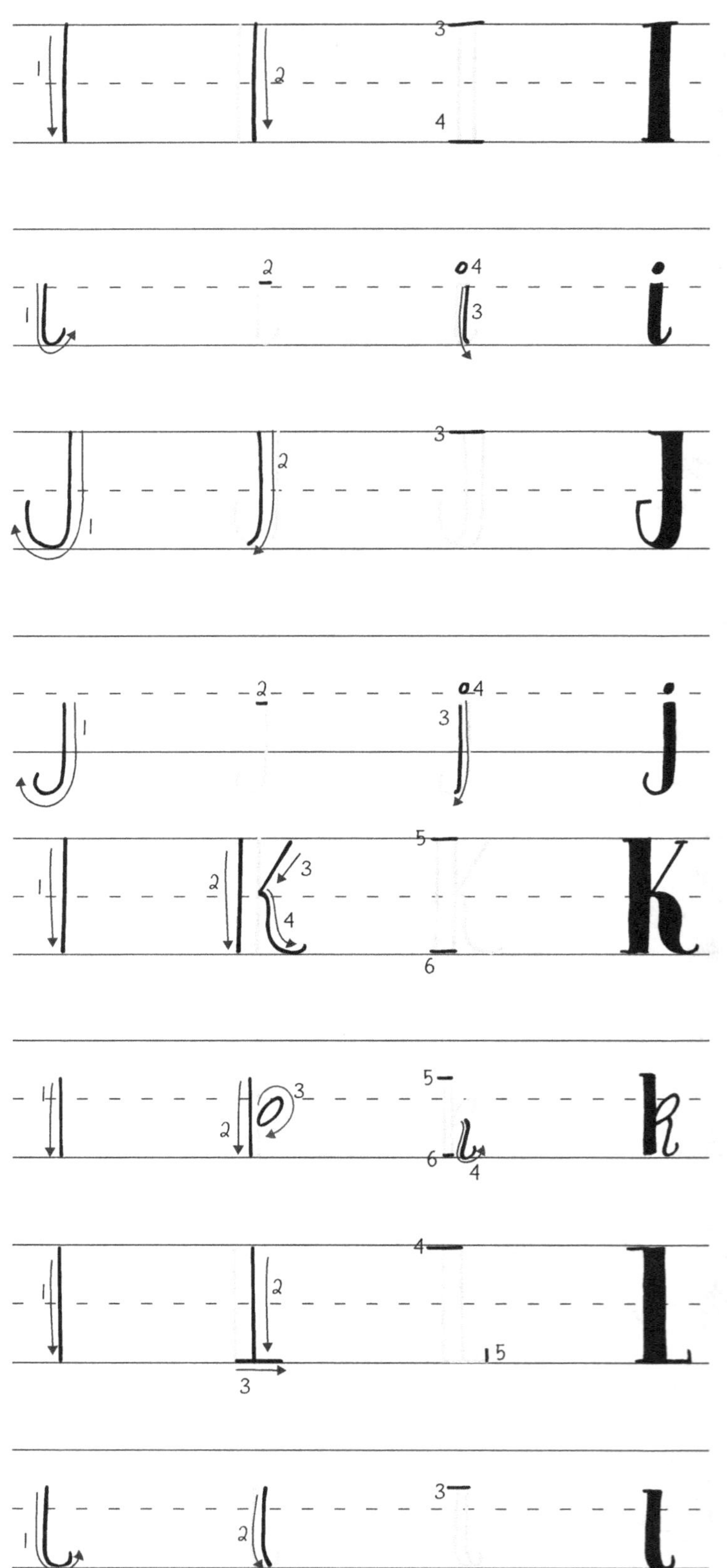

Ii Ii Ii Ii Ii Ii

Ii

Jj Jj Jj Jj Jj Jj

Jj

Kk Kk Kk Kk Kk Kk

Kk

Ll Ll Ll Ll Ll Ll

Ll

Mm

Nn

Oo

Pp

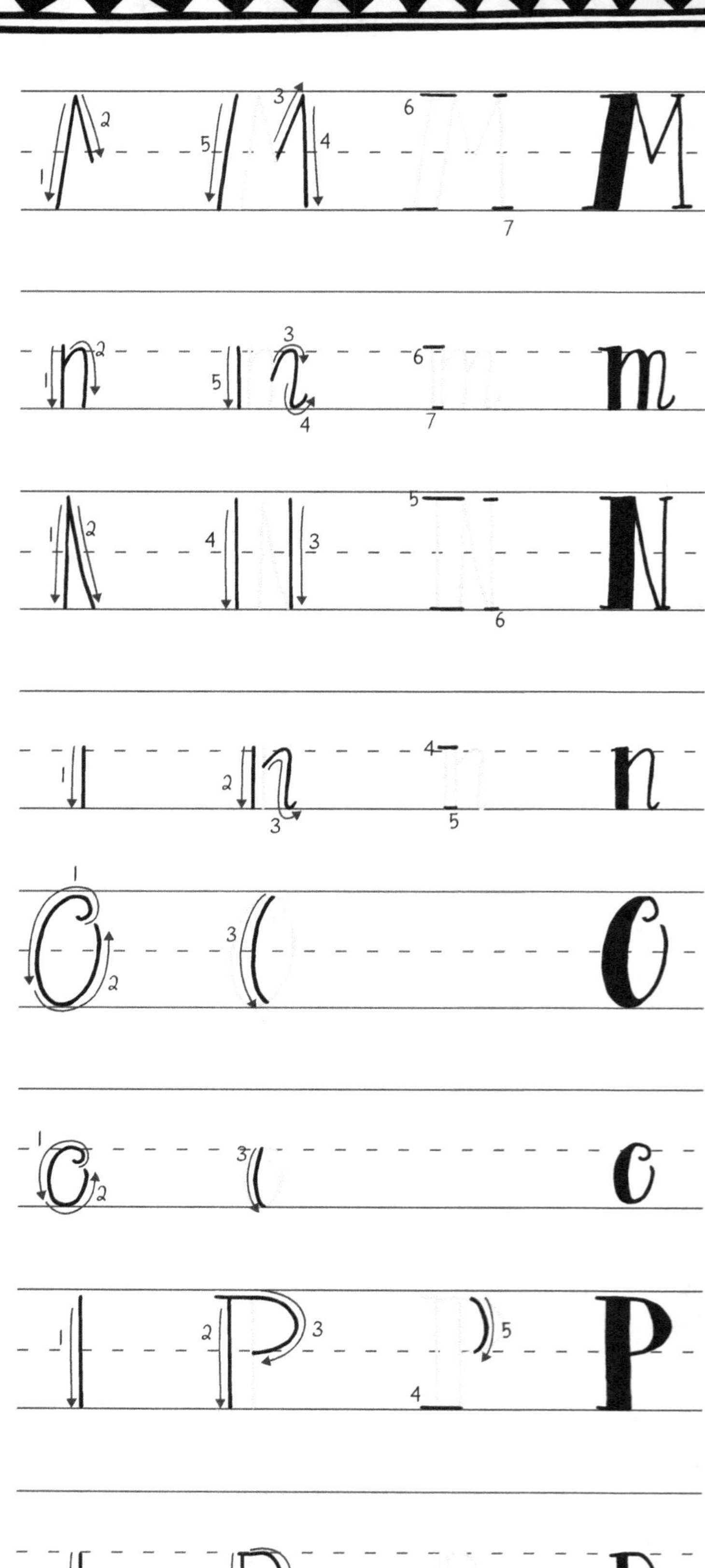

Qq

Rr

Ss

Tt

Qq Qq Qq Qq Qq Qq

Qq

Rr Rr Rr Rr Rr Rr

Rr

Ss Ss Ss Ss Ss Ss

Ss

Tt Tt Tt Tt Tt Tt

Tt

Uu

Vv

Ww

Xx

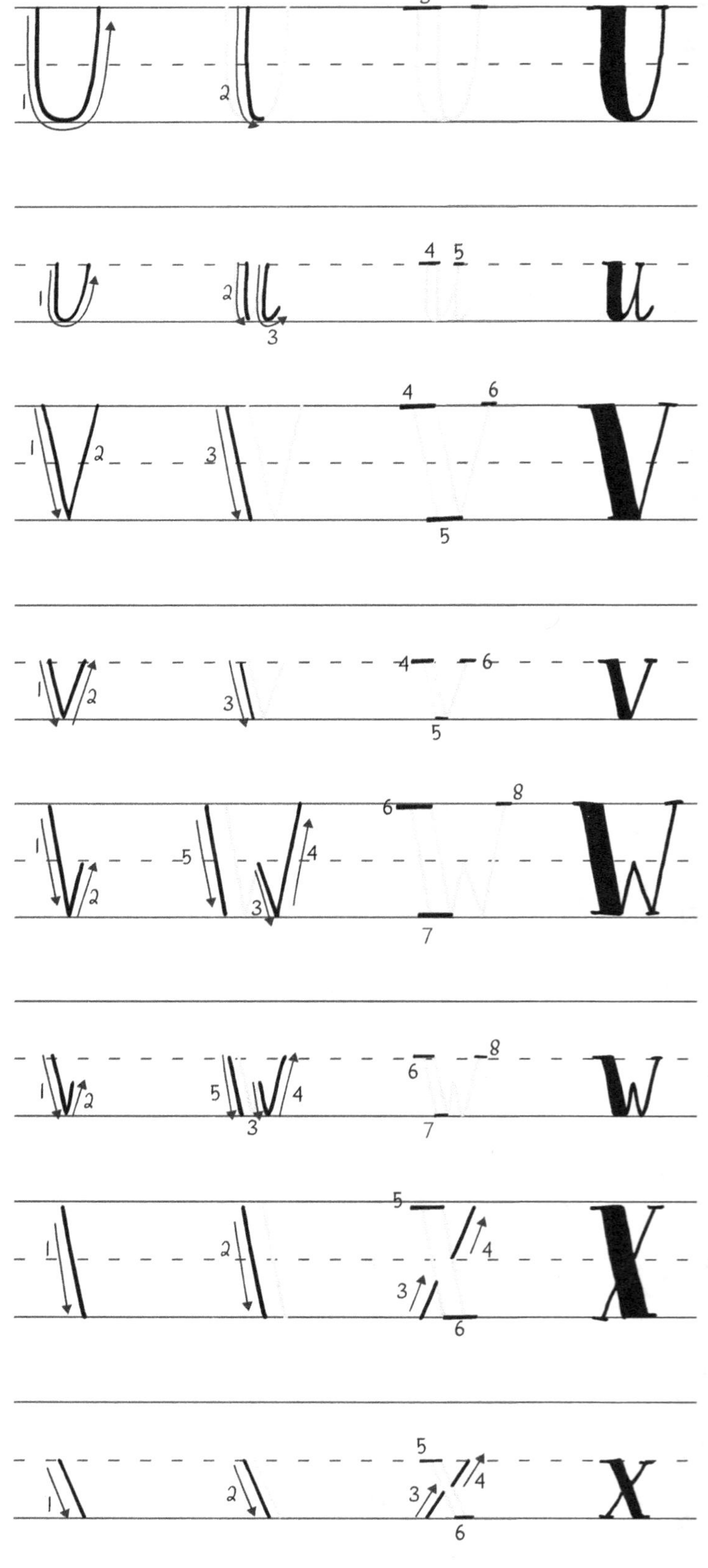

Uu Uu Uu Uu Uu Uu

Uu

Vv Vv Vv Vv Vv Vv

Vv

Ww Ww Ww Ww Ww Ww

Ww

Xx Xx Xx Xx Xx Xx

Xx

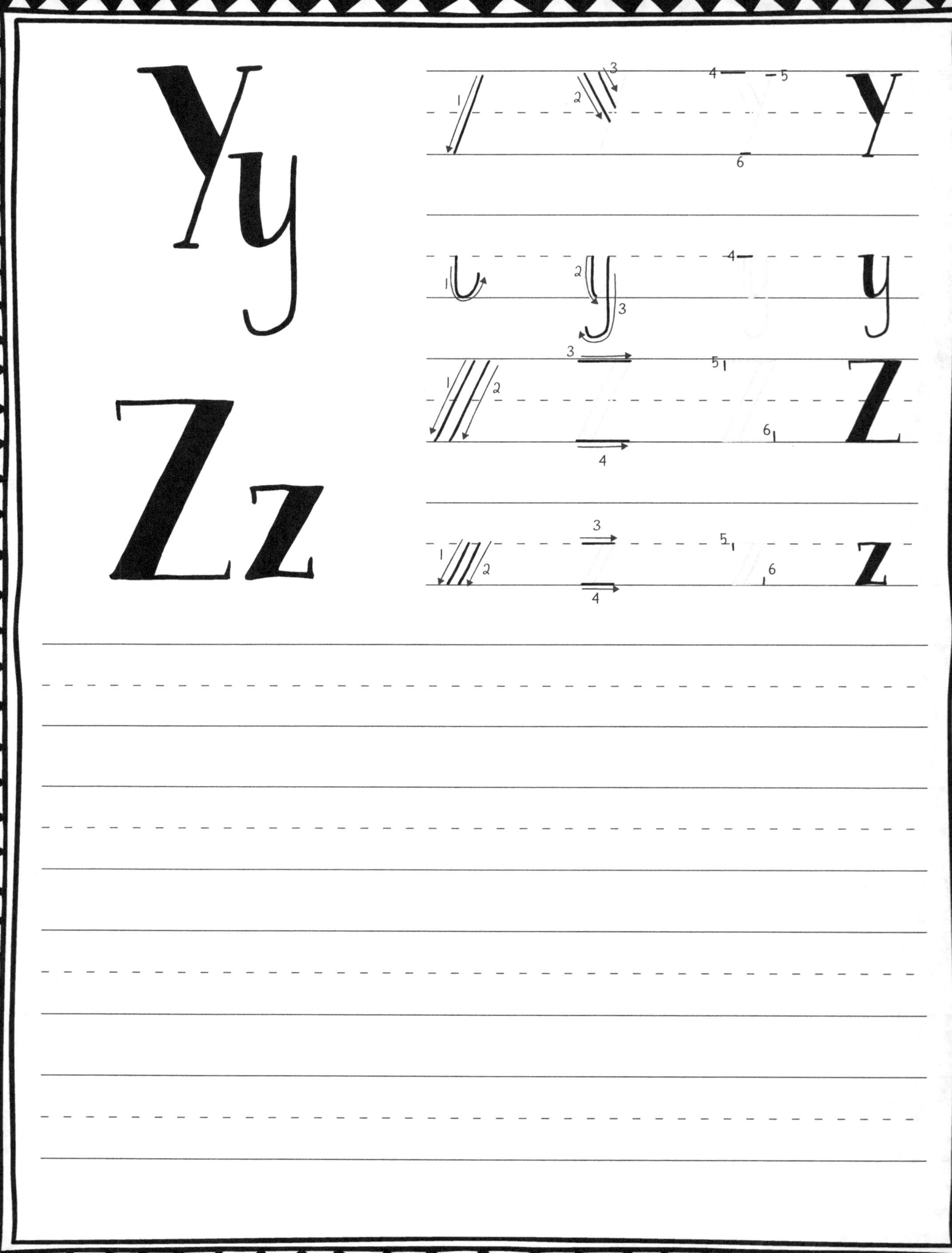

Yy
Zz

Yy Yy Yy Yy Yy Yy

Yy

Zz Zz Zz Zz Zz Zz

Zz

# CONNECTING LETTERS

Connected letters have a beautiful, flowing look and are super fun to do. Like all good things, this takes practice, so keep at it!

Different lettering styles have some rules surrounding connecting letters. For example, script letters are connected. Sans Serif and Serif are not connected at all.

Let me explain this process to you guys in a bit more detail. See the lovely connected word 'banana' below?

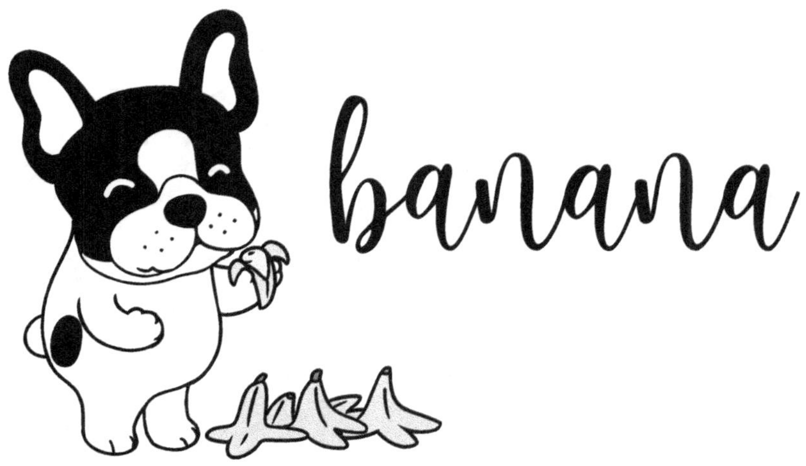


Can you see how each connection of letters is the same length and shape? Note how the spacing between the letters is nice and even. It's important to keep those connections consistent and matching. Remember that the end upstroke is always the stroke that connects to the next letter.

See how the ending upstroke is connecting to the next letter

Also, it helps a lot to think ahead about which letter you'll be writing next so that the flow keeps going without you stopping and wondering what's next and interrupting that nice connection.

If you've connected letters before, you'll have noticed how some letters just naturally flow into the next one easily, but others just don't. In those cases, try a few different ways to connect them and choose your favorite.

See below letters:

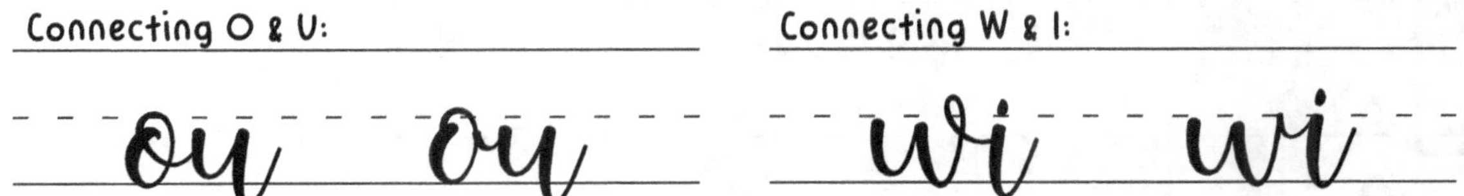


Using loops to connect the letters is fun, but keep in mind that too many loops can make it look a bit messy and difficult to read each letter.

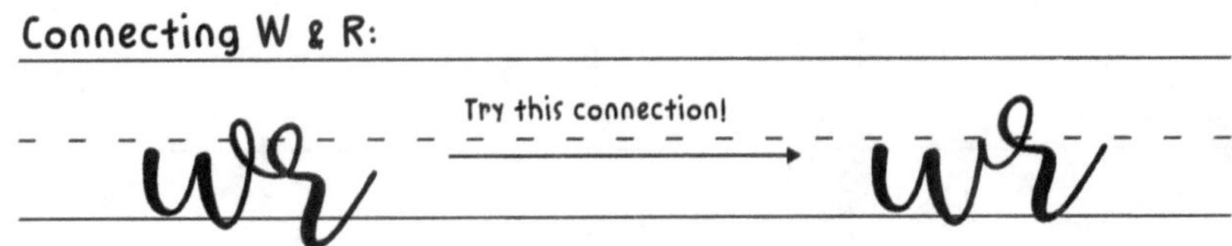


Oh, and you know what? You don't even need to connect each letter! If it feels too forced and looks unnatural being connected, simply leave that letter as it is.

On the next few pages, try to connect the monoline letter first, then try the hand-lettered script later where you can work on the thickness and pressure of the downstroke.

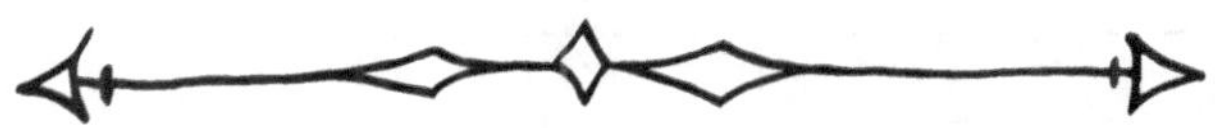

joy

true

rise

star

wish

smile

sweet

spring

home home

world world

curious curious

imagine imagine

precious precious

sunshine sunshine

lemonade lemonade

Christmas Christmas

sky sky

life life

mind mind

love love

kind kind

bliss bliss

magic magic

bloom bloom

dream dream

perfect perfect

blessings blessings

summer summer

positive positive

laughs laughs

strength strength

grateful grateful

# MAKE YOUR LETTERS EXTRA-SPECIAL!

Okay, we're really going to start getting creative here.

See if you can copy the word below, working on your pressure and joining the letters carefully. Make sure you're confident with this word before moving on to the next stage.

Original

love

Now, you're going to add some shadow lines:

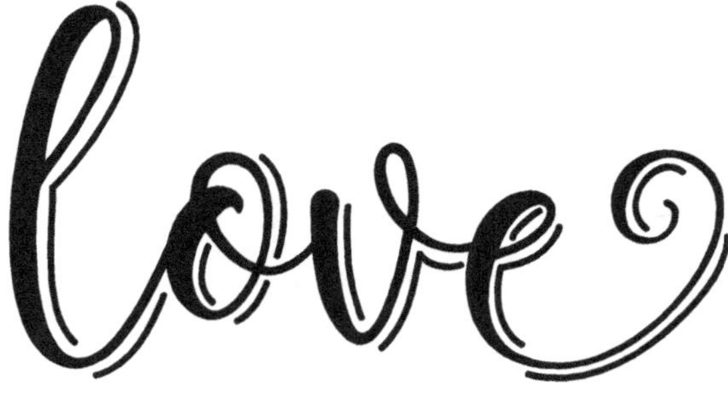

Try to add some highlights with a white gel pen!

love

Try stretching out the letters this time. What a difference, hey!

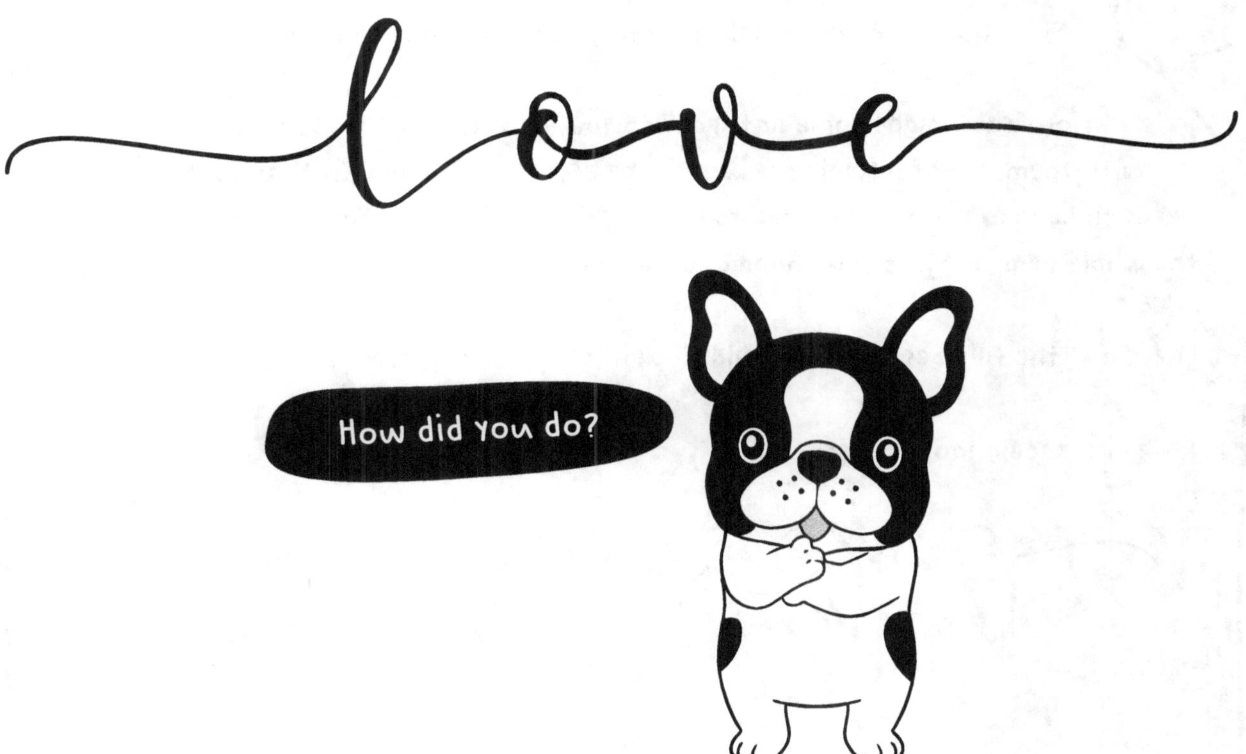


Now, it's time to find your own style! Maybe you'd like to try squishing up the letters? Or stretching the letters out even more.

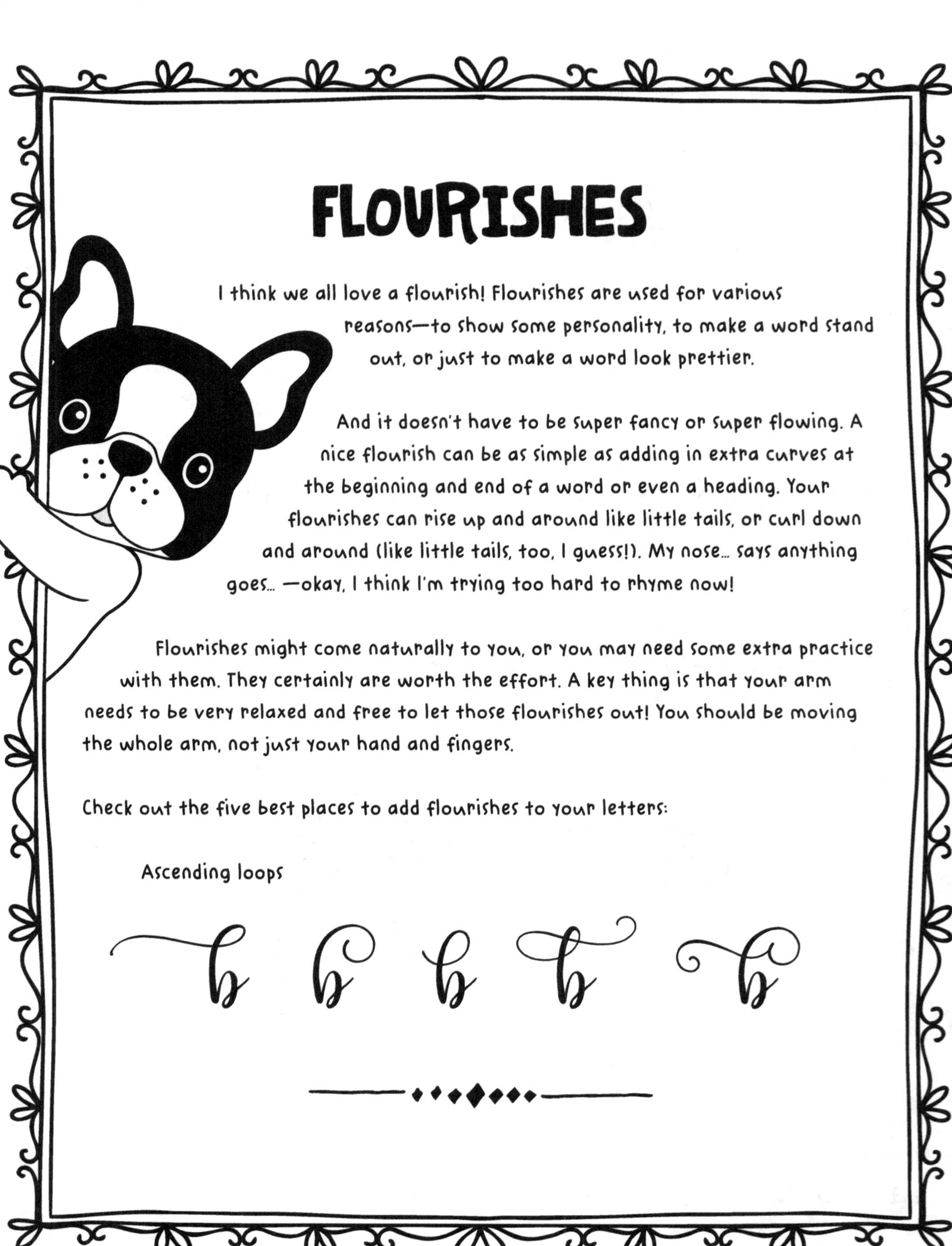

# FLOURISHES

I think we all love a flourish! Flourishes are used for various reasons—to show some personality, to make a word stand out, or just to make a word look prettier.

And it doesn't have to be super fancy or super flowing. A nice flourish can be as simple as adding in extra curves at the beginning and end of a word or even a heading. Your flourishes can rise up and around like little tails, or curl down and around (like little tails, too, I guess!). My nose… says anything goes… —okay, I think I'm trying too hard to rhyme now!

Flourishes might come naturally to you, or you may need some extra practice with them. They certainly are worth the effort. A key thing is that your arm needs to be very relaxed and free to let those flourishes out! You should be moving the whole arm, not just your hand and fingers.

Check out the five best places to add flourishes to your letters:

Ascending loops

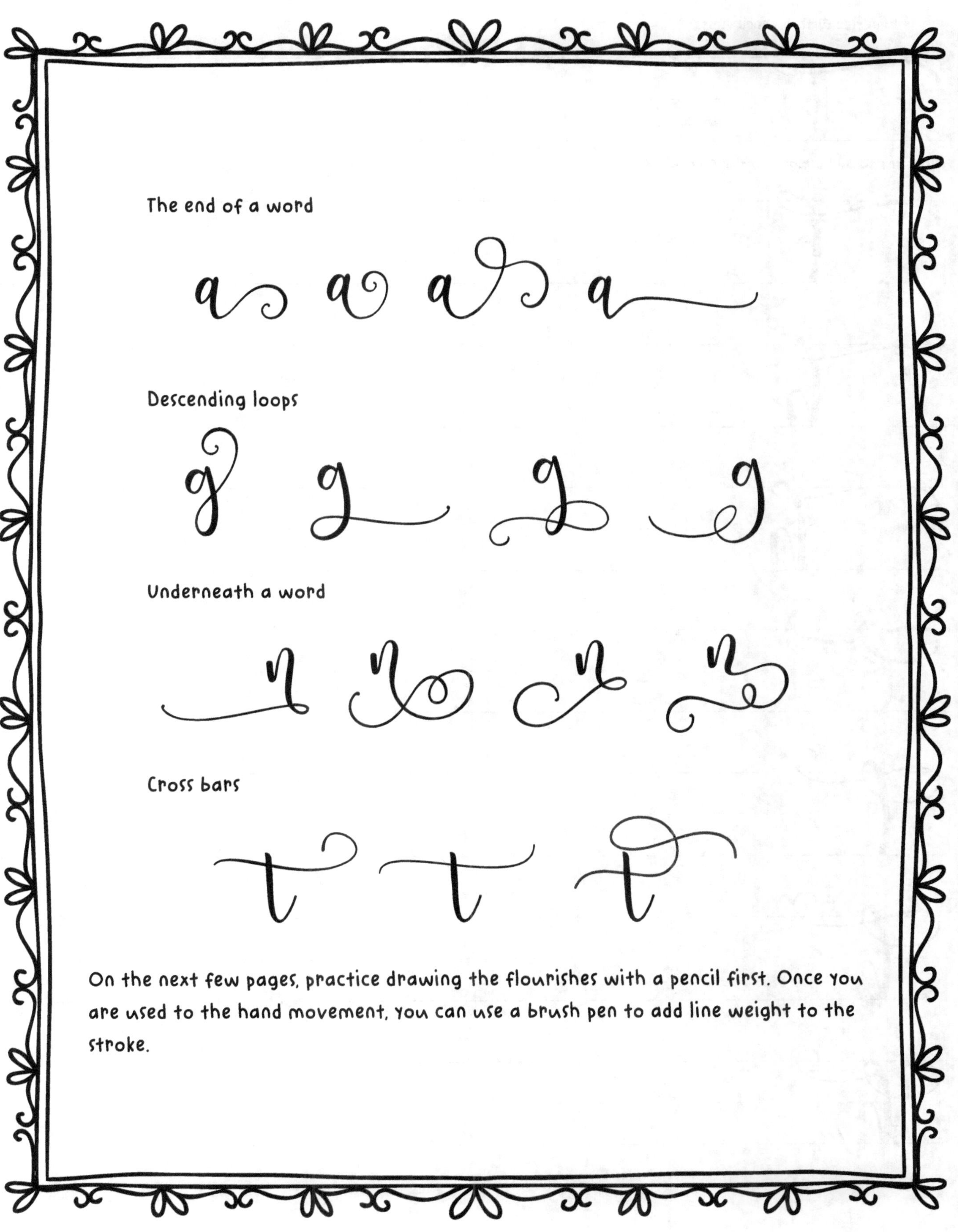


On the next few pages, practice drawing the flourishes with a pencil first. Once you are used to the hand movement, you can use a brush pen to add line weight to the stroke.

## Flourishes

Practice with a pencil first.

Now try to add weight to the stroke.

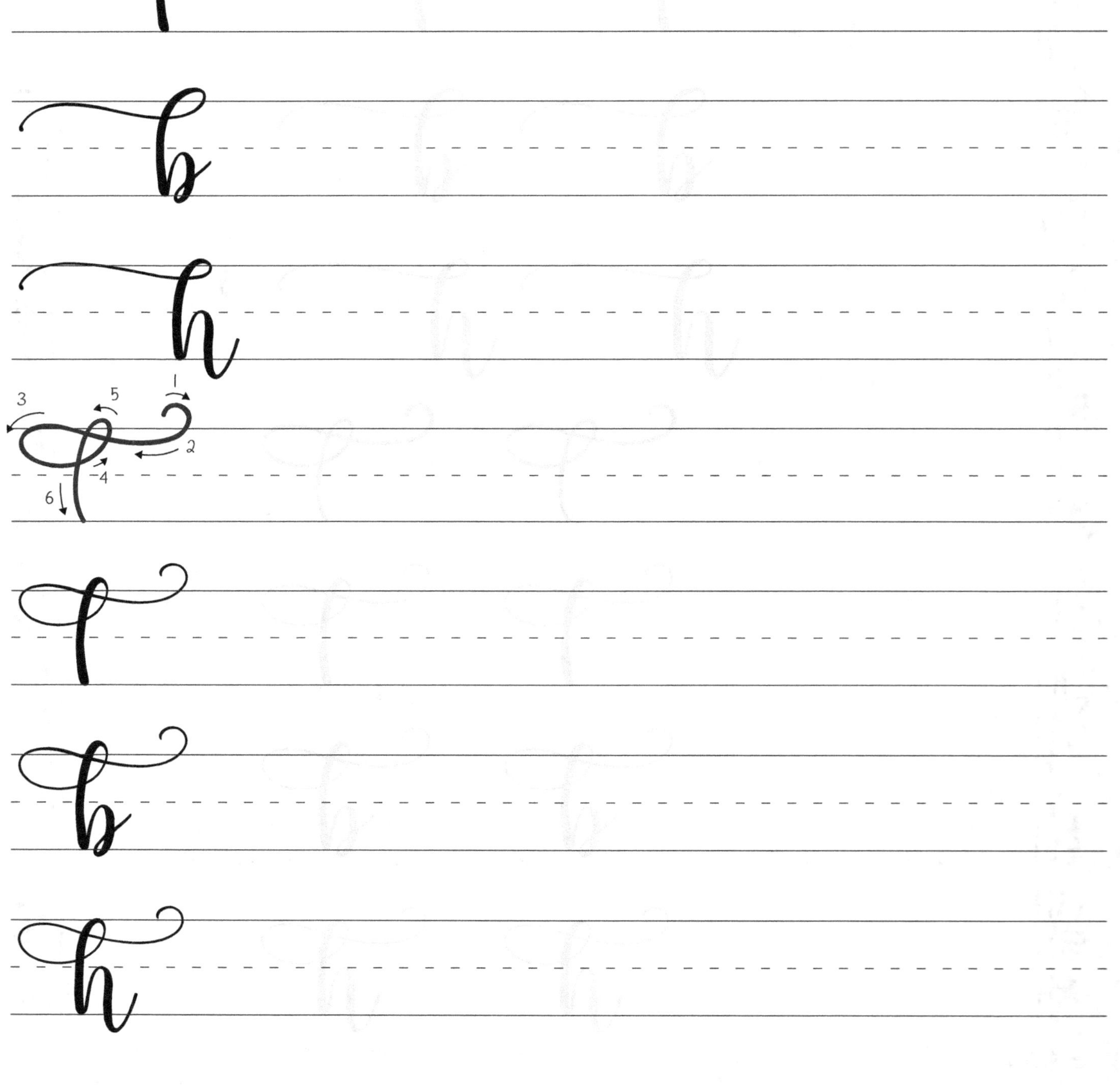

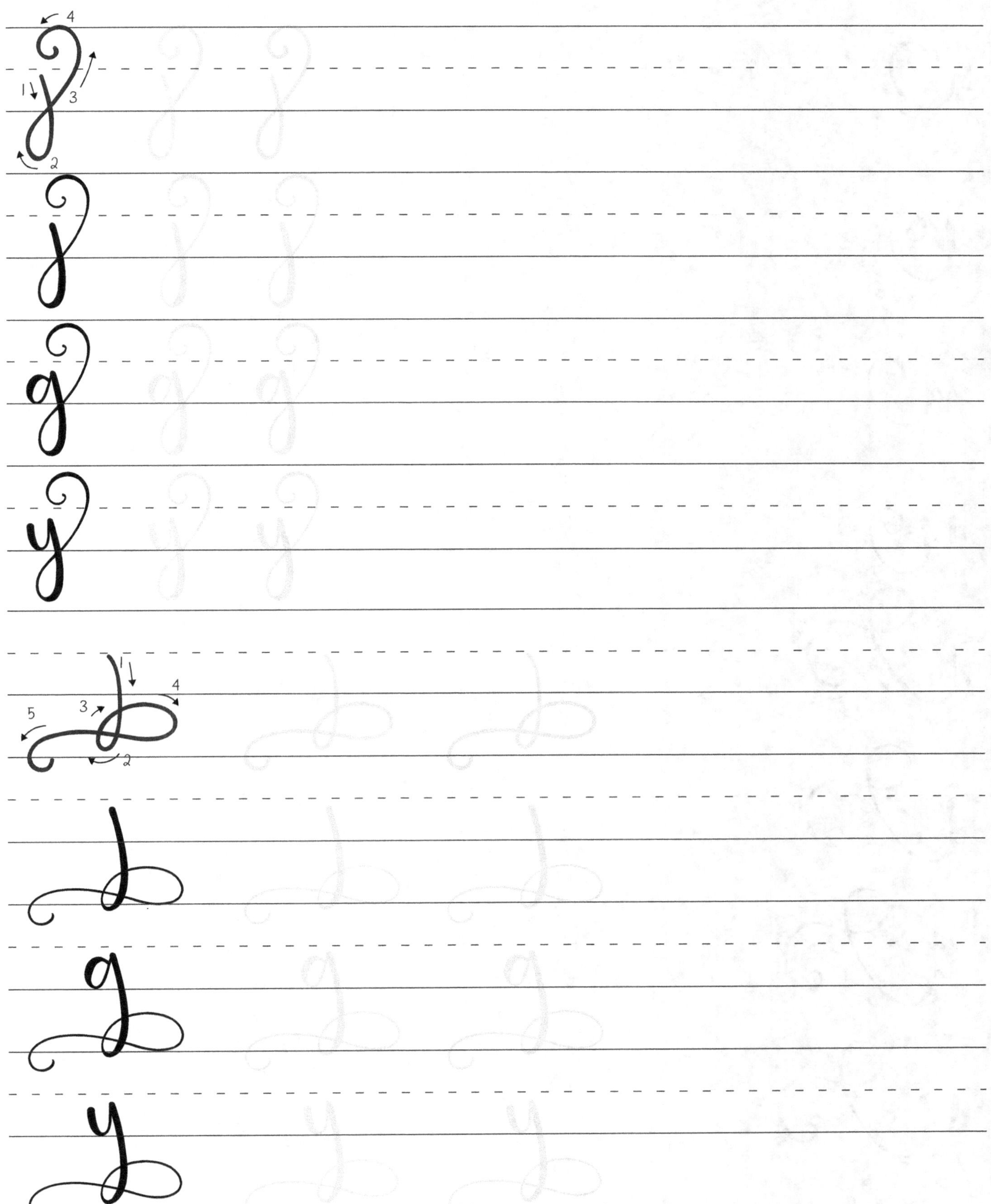

# Flourishes

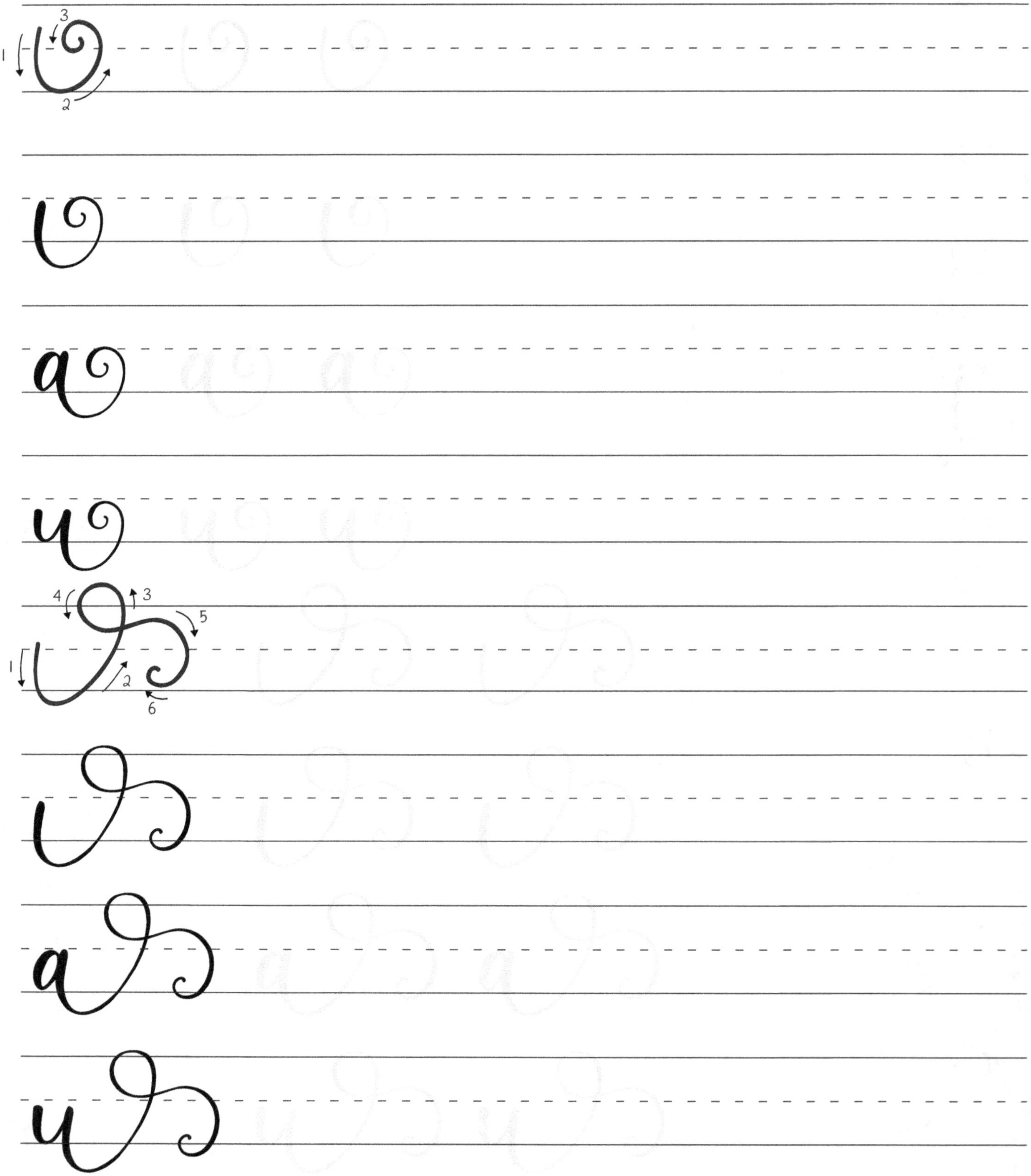

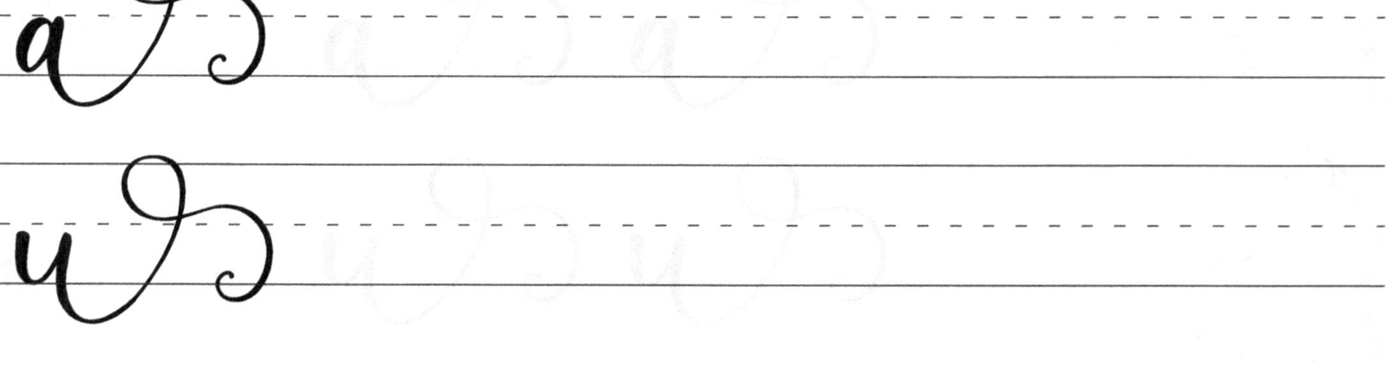

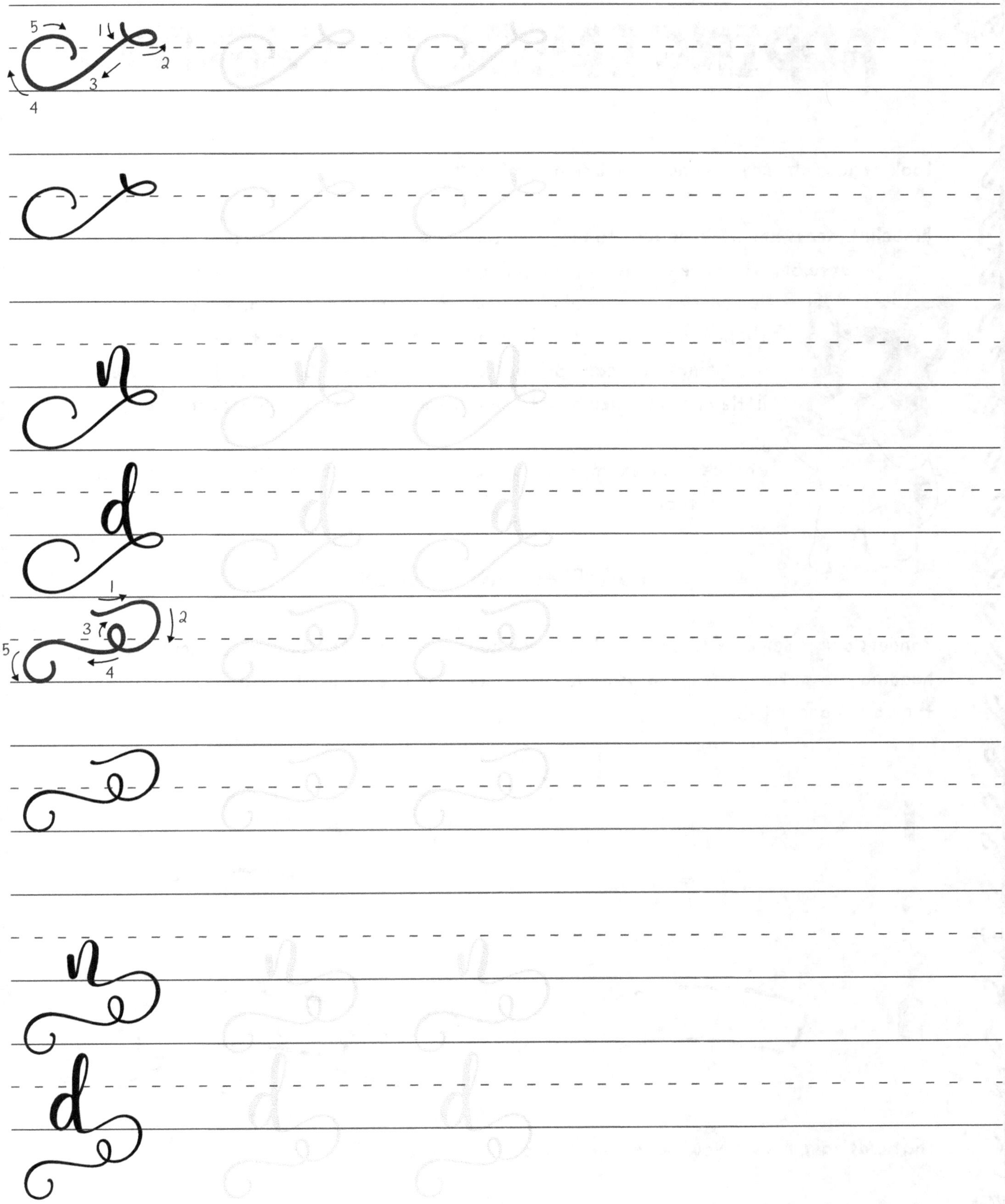

5 1 2 3 4

n

d

1 2 3 5 4

n

d

# ADDING EMBELLISHMENT!

Look at you, already advancing to adding embellishments!

Embellishments are little designs to brighten up and add detail to your writing, a logo, or artwork. They are also handy for filling in some blank spaces, adding personality or elements of a particular theme, (for example adding some stars to a theme on space or star signs, or adding little flowers to a card celebrating spring). You can add your own squiggles or swirls, maybe some cute little drawings like hearts, mini sushi, a cat's face—whatever you like.

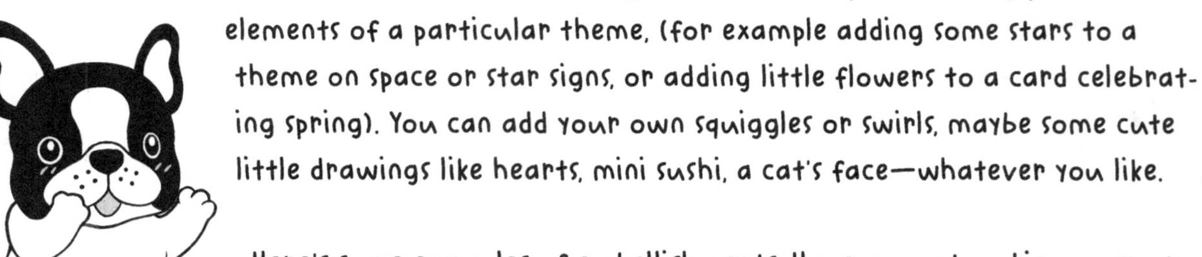

Here's some examples of embellishments. Have a go at making up your own, too!

## HOW TO DRAW BANNERS

Banners are super easy to do, but they really do look impressive! They can be great for headings or making certain parts of your writing stand out. First, have a go at drawing the basic banner below.

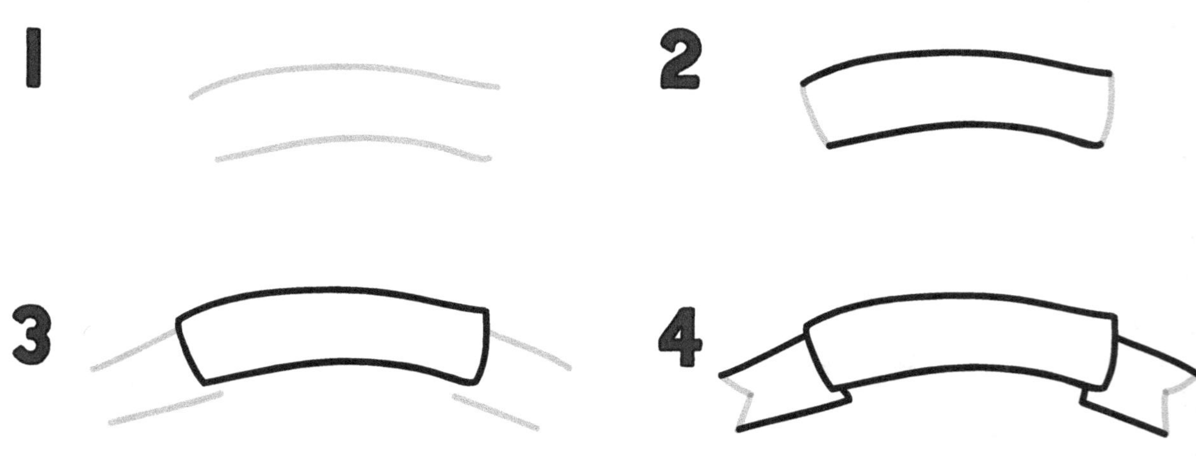


That was easy, right? Now have a go at a double banner.

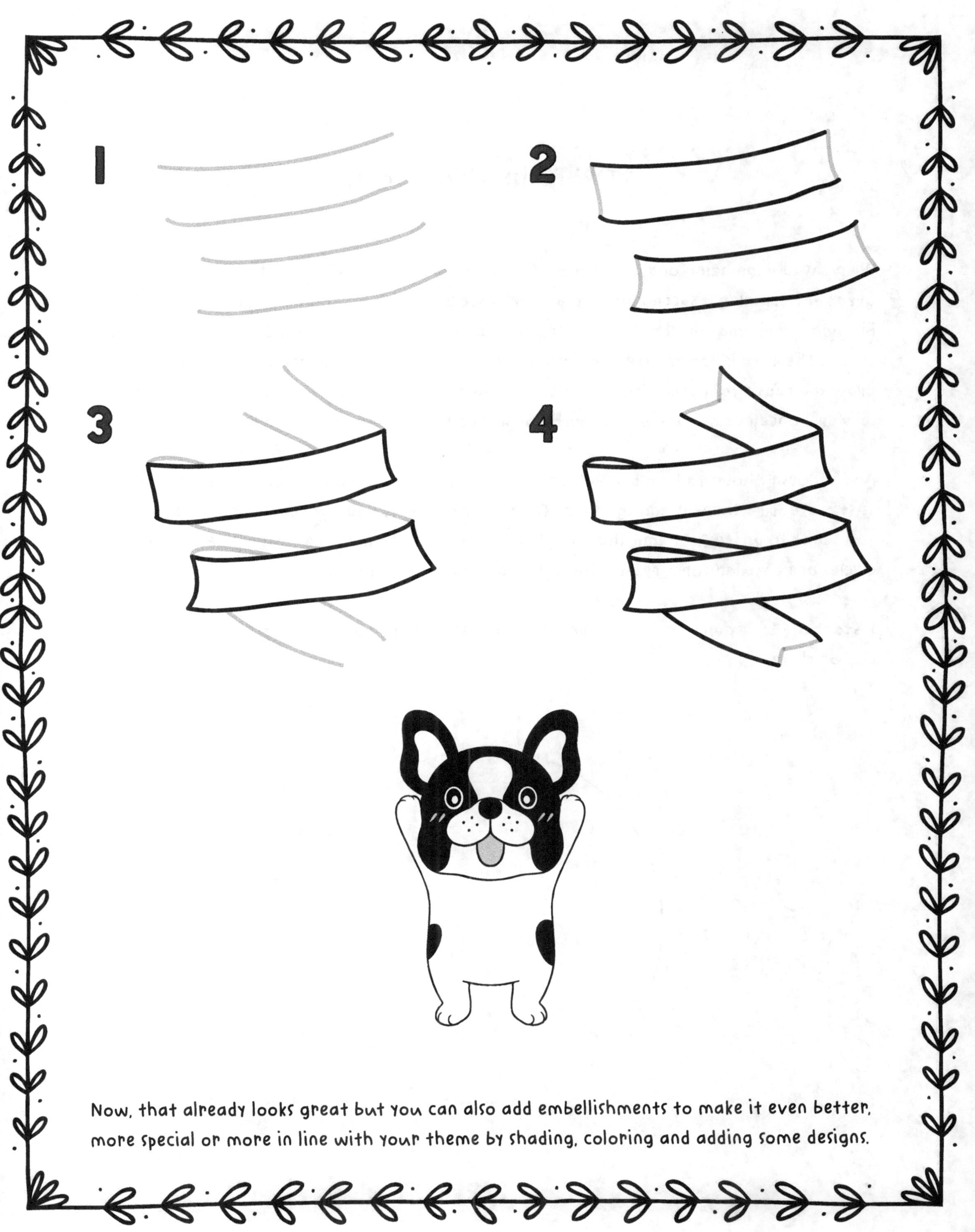


Now, that already looks great but you can also add embellishments to make it even better, more special or more in line with your theme by shading, coloring and adding some designs.

# HOW TO DRAW A WREATH

Wreaths look amazing and are perfect for framing your new skill of lettering! They are great for framing a special word, a phrase, a special picture or name. They are great on birthday, Christmas or thank-you cards, too. Design the wreath around the theme or the person the card is for. Maybe they love flowers, or cooking, or forest animals? You can draw a wreath to match the season, such as autumn leaves for autumn or snowflakes for winter. I once even saw a wreath with skulls and roses, so anything goes!

And it doesn't have to be a perfect circle. It could be an oval, half-circle or heart-shaped. Just make sure there is enough space for your hand lettering in the middle, so plan what you want to write first, and that will tell you what size and shape you will need. Floral circles are popular for a reason though—they do look beautiful!

1. Start off by drawing a circle in pencil using a stencil or protractor. You could even use a cup or plate!

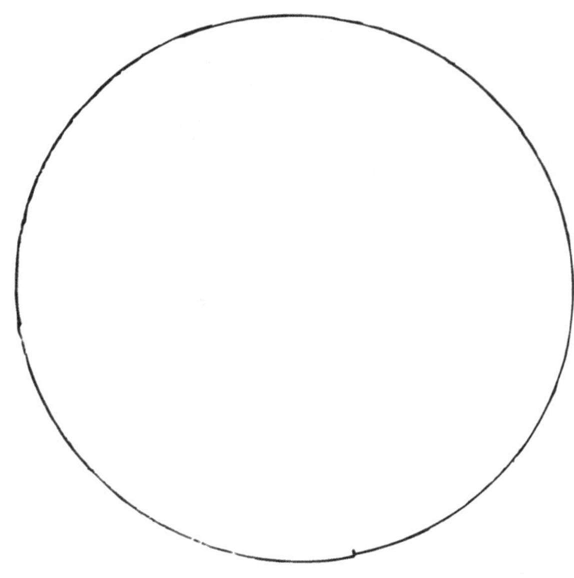

2. Next, draw four lines to divide your circle up into eight sections—one horizontal (across) and one vertical (down the middle) and two diagonal (across). And don't worry-it doesn't have to be perfectly even. It will just help balance out your wreath.

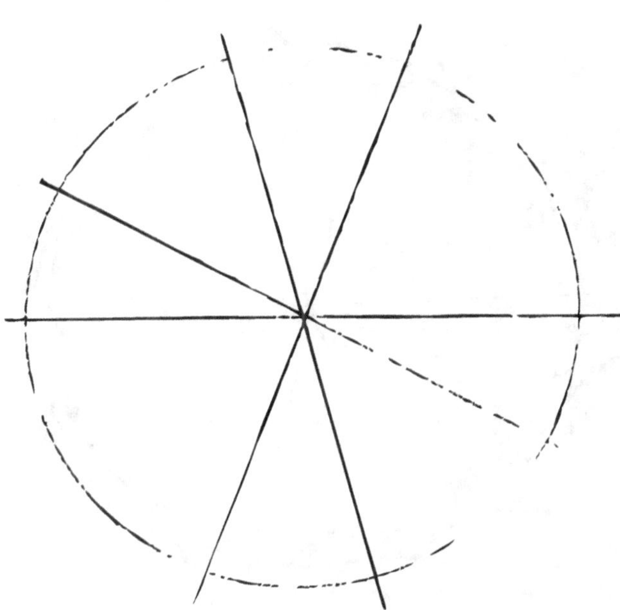

3. Now, with a fineliner, you can add the 'stems' of your wreath. Each section has two or three stems. There are no rules here, but it's easier to stick to these basics while you're getting the hang of it. See below:

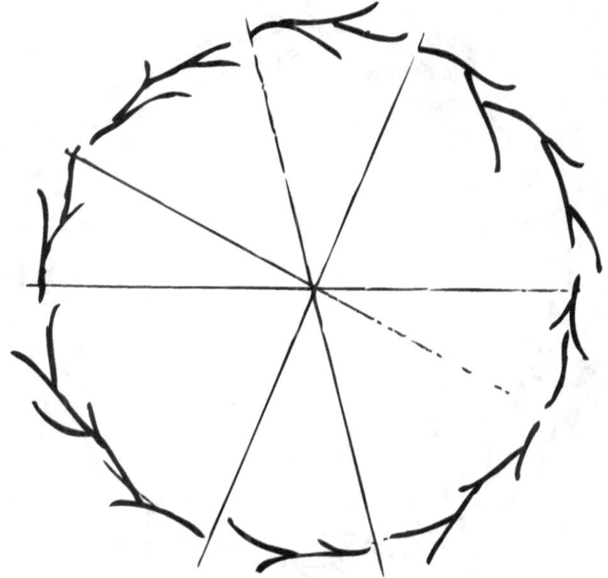

4. Now, start off by adding little leaves and flowers to the end of those stems. You're having fun, I know it!

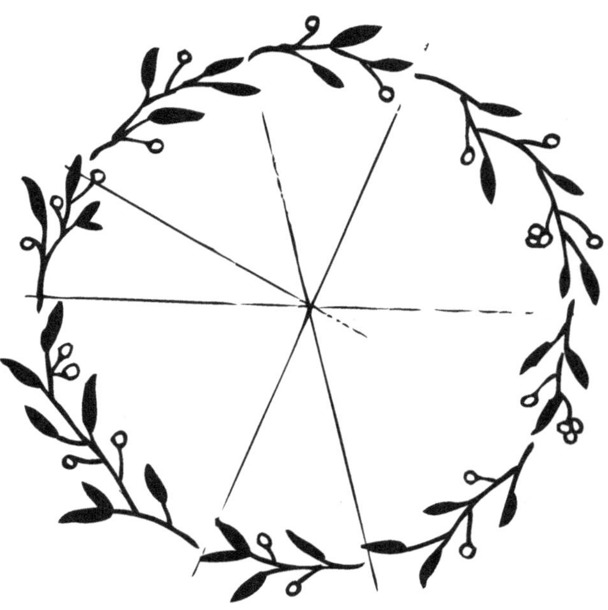

5. Is it looking great? I bet it is. Don't forget to erase your pencil lines here.

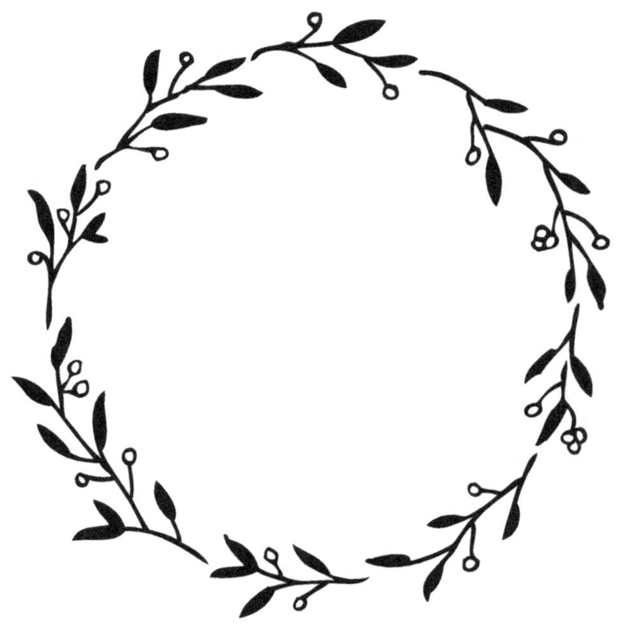

Check out these other examples using the same process you did above but with some variations. See the added flower?

And here, the wreath is left open which can come in handy when you need a lot of space for text:

Why not add a banner to the top or bottom? (You banner expert, you!)

I say the best designs are your own. Trust your own ideas! Don't overthink them. Just let them pour out of your arm, no matter if it feels silly. See what pops out! But on the next page are some ideas to get you started for the next birthday card. Remember to think about who it is for and make it special for them choosing designs and colors to match their personality or your friendship.

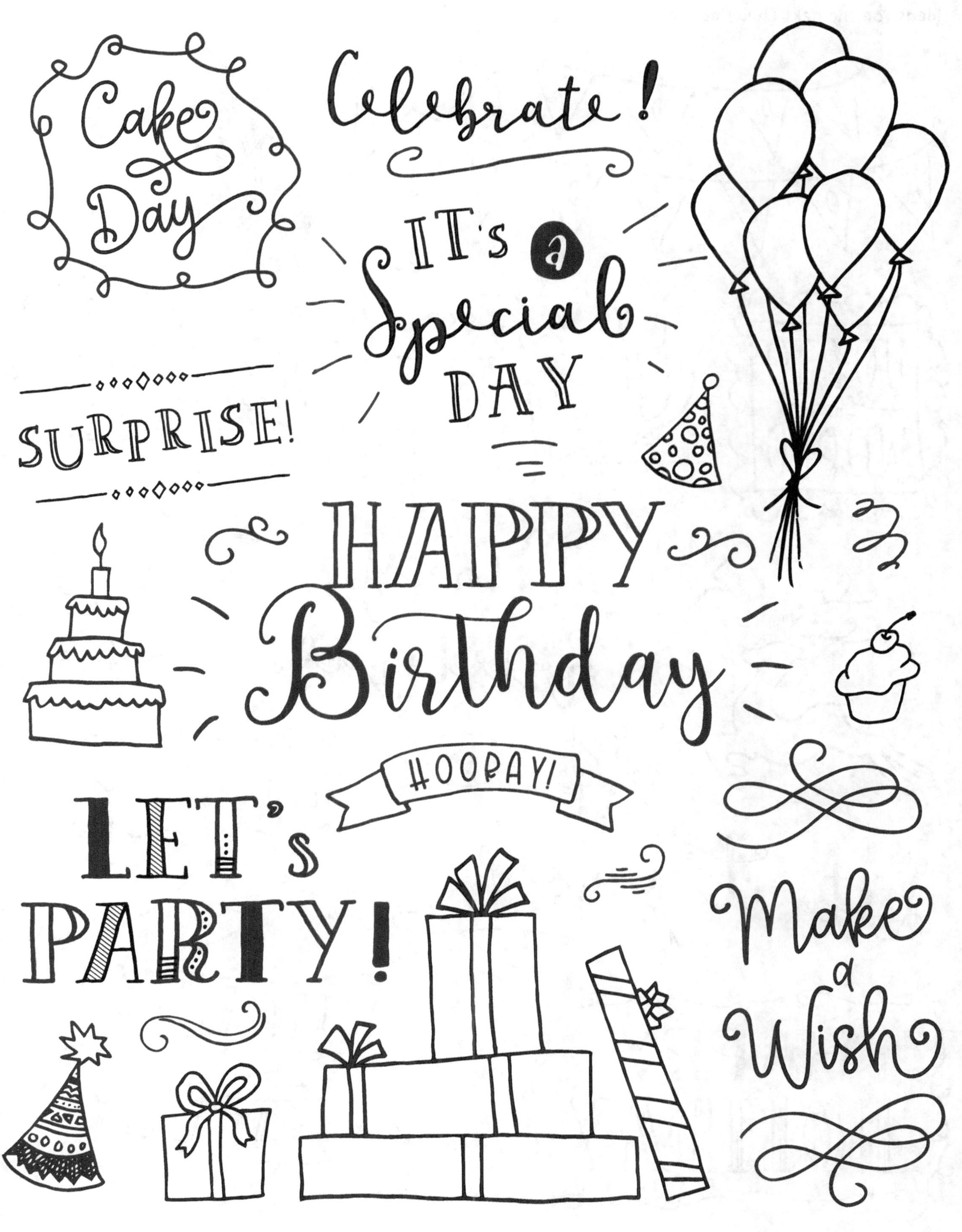
Cake Day
Celebrate!
IT's a Special DAY
SURPRISE!
HAPPY Birthday
HOORAY!
LET's PARTY!
Make a Wish

Ideas for the next Christmas card:

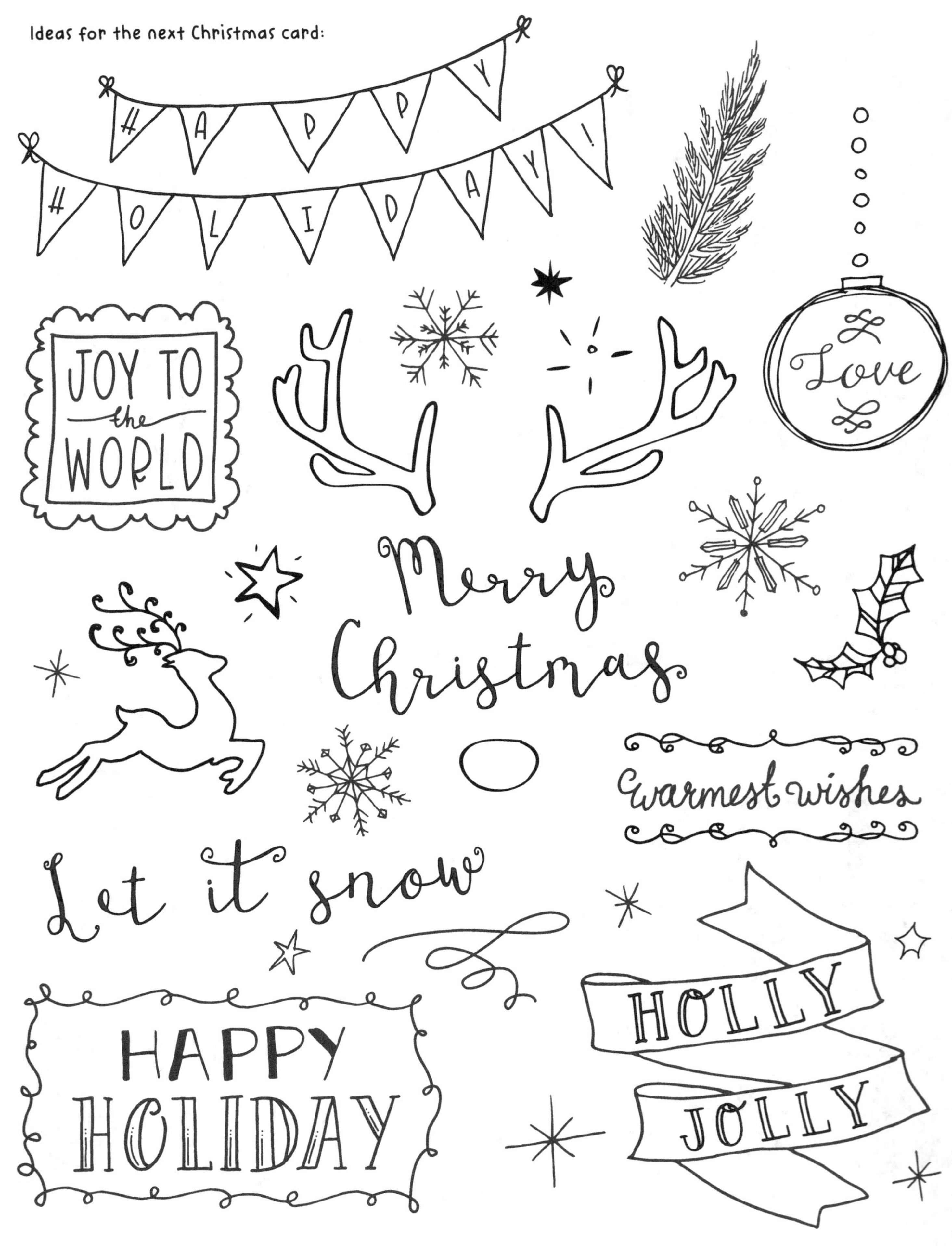

# GUESS WHAT? YOU'RE AWESOME!

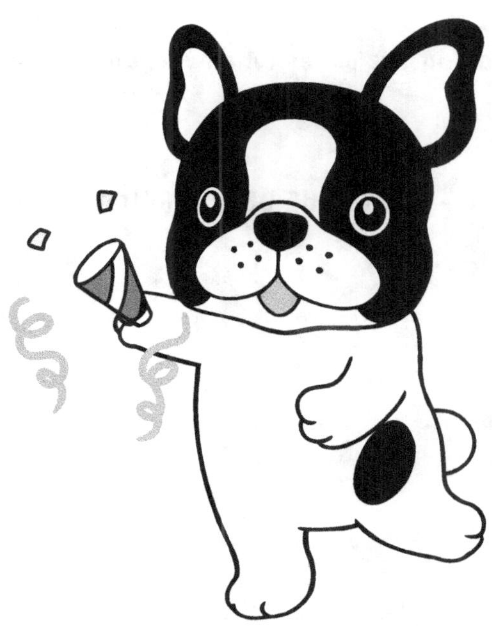

It's over to you, awesome one! How do I know you're awesome? Well, you've made it this far and are now a skilled hand letterer. Awesome! And, you bought this book written by me—pawsome!

Now's the time to let your awesomeness (Oh, have I done it again? Is that a word? Well, it is now!) out and use everything you've learned to develop your own unique style that is awesomely (?) you. I think I'm going overboard with the awesome. Okay, so why not feel 'great' while copying out these positive quotes below? Then have a go at making up your own. Once you're done, you might like to place it somewhere you see every day as a happy reminder. Or maybe you'd like to write a card for someone special in your life who needs a reminder that they are awesome too?

# YOU'RE A GEM!

You are a gem! You're very special, like a shining gem, and don't forget it! But in case you do forget, draw this one, go on! The lettering style below is a mix of Monoline and Serif with some lovely flourishes and embellishment.

Tip: Try not to rest your hand on the paper when you are drawing, otherwise the line might not be smooth.

TRACE THE DESIGN BELOW

PRACTICE AGAIN HERE

# BELIEVE IN YOURSELF

Do you believe that you can do anything you want to? That you have it all inside you? Well, it's time to start!

Draw the main keywords first (believe and yourself). Then fill in the serif letters.

TRACE THE DESIGN BELOW

Believe IN Yourself

PRACTICE AGAIN HERE

# NOTHING IS IMPOSSIBLE

Sometimes we might doubt whether we can do something. It could be something new, or something we're a bit afraid of. But if you practice and try hard and 'believe in yourself' (see above!) then absolutely nothing is impossible.

You can practice drawing the flourish for 'g' with a pencil first.

TRACE THE DESIGN BELOW

Nothing
is
Impossible

PRACTICE AGAIN HERE

# MAKE IT HAPPEN

It would be nice if they did, but things don't just happen by themselves. We need to take action to make things we want in our lives to happen. Maybe you want to own a new bike. Start working, start saving—make it happen!

Write the Serif first. Then add the 'it' with as much or as little flourish as you like. Add the embellishment last.

TRACE THE DESIGN BELOW

MAKE
it
HAPPEN

PRACTICE AGAIN HERE

# EMBRACE THE JOURNEY

Are you planning a trip to the beach? Do you just want to jump in the water right now? That's fair enough, but don't waste the car journey feeling impatient and arguing with your siblings. Embrace the journey! Don't feel frustrated while learning hand lettering. Embrace the journey of practicing!

Draw the keywords first for this one, too. Remember to lift your pen up after each stroke to have better control.

TRACE THE DESIGN BELOW

Embrace
THE
Journey

PRACTICE AGAIN HERE

# YOU'RE FREE TO FLY

Don't let anyone hold you back from your dreams. Your dreams are your dreams. Feel free to fly, reach for the stars!

For this one, get those curves below right first (just like your banners) and then fill them in with your words. Add some fun embellishments last.

TRACE THE DESIGN BELOW

YOU'RE FREE TO FLY

PRACTICE AGAIN HERE

# YOU'VE GOT THAT SPECIAL SOMETHING

Everyone has a special 'something' or skill. Yours might be hand lettering! But it might not, and that's okay. Try lots of different things, be open to new experiences, and you will find your 'special something' when the time is right.

Draw the keywords first. Add the other words in the space that's left (I hope you left some space!) Remember, go slow!

TRACE THE DESIGN BELOW

You've
GOT THAT
Special
SOMETHING

PRACTICE AGAIN HERE

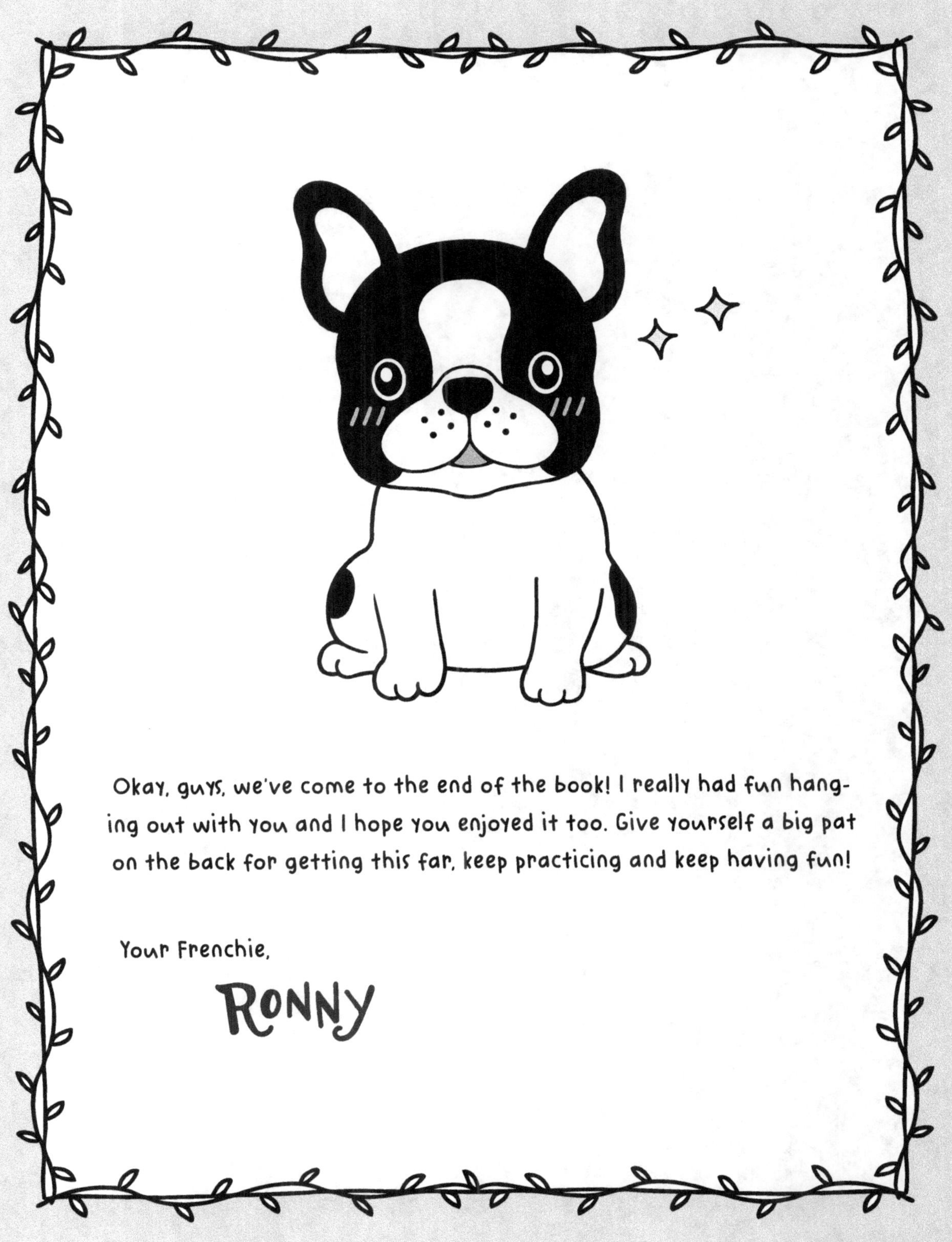

Okay, guys, we've come to the end of the book! I really had fun hanging out with you and I hope you enjoyed it too. Give yourself a big pat on the back for getting this far, keep practicing and keep having fun!

Your Frenchie,

RONNY

www.ingramcontent.com/pod-product-compliance
Lightning Source LLC
Chambersburg PA
CBHW080516030726
47592CB00012B/3363